Michigan's
Guide to Local Cooking

~ *by* Susan Clemente ~

orange whisk

CREDITS & ACKNOWLEDGEMENTS:

Author: Susan Clemente
Editor: Merrie Campbell-Lee
Editor: Mary Clemente

Art & Photography: Susan Clemente

Special thanks to Michigan's small farmers and purveyors
that provide us with healthy foods.

TEXT COPYRIGHT ©2011 Susan Clemente
COVER PHOTOGRAPHY ©Liza McCorkle
PHOTOGRAPHY COPYRIGHT ©2011 Susan Clemente

ISBN-10: 0-615-40003-5
ISBN-13: 9780615400037

Library of Congress Control Number: 2011921047

PUBLISHED BY:

Orange Whisk Books
P.O. Box 60
Spring Lake, MI 49456

WWW.ORANGEWHISKBOOKS.COM

printed in
Michigan

Cooper, F. G. [c. 1914-1918]. *Food...Don't Waste It.* U.S. Food Administration, (New York: W.F. Powers Litho.) Documenting the American South. University Library, The University of North Carolina at Chapel Hill, 2002.

Traveling through Michigan to document its beauty, food, and agriculture was an amazing experience. Thanks to all the passionate artisans, farmers, chefs and supporters who shared their valuable expertise and experience.

Special thanks to my family and friends who encouraged and supported this project.

To my father, who taught me the value of fresh food.
To my mother, who never doubted and fully supported writing this book.
To my grandmother, who introduced me to cooking with community.

table of CONTENTS

Michigan's summer and fall seasons provide the perfect climate for a bounty of fresh local foods. Produce can be grown in a garden or purchased from farmers markets, farm stands, or community supported agriculture programs (CSAs). The state has an abundance of dairy, poultry, and livestock farms that produce fresh milk, cheese, and eggs, as well as chicken, turkey, beef, pork, buffalo and lamb. Commercial and sport fishing in lakes and streams also provides a variety of delicious fresh water fish.

Small Michigan farmers, organic or otherwise, usually demonstrate a high regard for the environment through the use of crop rotations, while also utilizing organic matter for fertilizer. Such practices reduce the use of petroleum-based fertilizers and pesticides. Purchasing foods from these local farmers is not only healthier for you and your family, but also improves the environment by reducing the miles your food has traveled, which reduces your carbon footprint.

In addition, it is economically advantageous to support local farmers and retailers. Small local businesses positively impact our communities and small business owners bring character to our neighborhoods as well as support community projects. Spending money at local businesses facilitates the employment of friends, and neighbors. Small businesses typically provide better customer service as well as greater product variety than big-box stores.

The purpose of this book is to increase awareness about food; where it originates, how it's grown, and how far it's traveled before it reaches your fork.

~ Thought for food ~

Chapter one discusses the differences between large-scale factory farming and small-scale local farming. It focuses on the production of our food, and how it affects our environment as well as our local economies.

Most fresh produce sold in your local supermarket was grown on factory farms and has traveled long distances to reach your table. Even though broccoli and carrots are likely grown within 20 miles of the average American's home, these vegetables have traveled an average of 1,800 miles to reach your local grocer.[1]

The majority of meat and poultry found in the supermarket comes from factory-farmed, feedlot-raised animals. This impacts the health of both you and the animal. According to the Center for Urban Education about Sustainable Agriculture, feedlot-raised animals are often fed an unnatural diet of corn, soy, antibiotics, and hormones, and, as a result, they grow abnormally fast.[2]

Meat, eggs, and dairy products from pastured, grass-fed animals are more nutritious. These products have more good fats, fewer bad fats, are richer in antioxidants, including vitamin E, beta-carotene, and vitamin C. Additionally, they do not contain traces of added hormones, antibiotics, or other drugs.[3] The meat from pasture-raised, grass-fed animals is lower in fat and calories than feedlot-raised animals. According to *The Journal of Animal Science*, "Grass-fed beef has the same amount of fat as a skinless chicken breast, wild deer, or elk. Research shows that lean beef actually lowers your 'bad' LDL cholesterol levels."[4]

According to the Environmental Protection Agency, factory farming is a major contributor to the pollution of our environment. Food production has become increasingly dependent on energy derived from fossil fuels for fertilizer production, crop irrigation, farm equipment processing, packaging and transportation. Trucking, shipping, and flying food around the globe reduces our air quality. For example, every year, nearly 270 million pounds of grapes arrive in California, most of them shipped from Chile to the Port of Los Angeles. Their 5,900-mile journey in both cargo ships and trucks releases 7,000 tons of carbon dioxide each year.[5]

Large-Scale Factory Farming

One benefit of large-scale factory farming is that food is grown cheaper and faster, creating higher product yields, giving more people access to fresh, inexpensive products. This is true for all sectors of the food industry including meat, poultry, and produce. Factory farming has created the biggest, fattest, juiciest pieces of meat and beautiful blemish-free vegetables and fruits. However, many of these factory-farmed foods are virtually tasteless when compared to farm fresh local foods. They are also pumped full of petroleum-based fertilizers and chemicals. These efforts to increase food production have actually produced food that is less nourishing. For more information on this topic, please review the article on page 17.

Most of the meat, eggs, and dairy products found in your local supermarket originate from animals raised in confinement in large factory-farming facilities or Confined Animal Feeding Operations (CAFOs). Conventional large-scale factory farms are designed to mass-produce food, not typically utilizing sustainable farming practices. Organic large-scale factory farms are required to follow the guidelines of the National Organic Program (NOP), which uses sustainable practices for both crop raising and animal rearing. However, many of the benefits of large-scale organic farming are lost because of the long distances the food is transported. Factory-farmed foods are marketed as being accessible and inexpensive, but the intrinsic cost associated with large-scale factory farming is damaging to our environment and our health.

A number of problems stem from large-scale factory farming, including the mistreatment of animals (stress and abuse), environmental pollution (air, water, and land), and loss of small farms and local businesses.

One concern of large-scale factory farming is **animal welfare**. Animals raised on factory farms are fed diets that are designed to boost their productivity at lower costs. The main feed ingredients can include "genetically modified corn and soy, which are kept at artificially low prices by government subsidies".[2] To cut costs further, feed producers may use a by-product feed such as municipal garbage as a filler.[2] Until 1997, U.S. cattle were also being fed meat that had been trimmed from other beef products, in effect turning herbivores into carnivores, which is believed to be the underlying cause of mad cow disease.[6]

A high-grain diet can also cause **physical problems** for cattle, dairy cows, goats, bison, and sheep because these animals naturally eat grasses and plants. To prevent more serious and sometimes fatal reactions, the animals are given chemical additives along with a low-level dose of antibiotics. Almost 75% of all antibiotics used in the United States today are used by CAFOs.[8]

Most of the nation's chickens, turkeys, and pigs are also raised in confinement, typically suffering more than the grazing animals.[2] Tightly packed into cages, sheds, or pens, they cannot practice their normal behaviors. Laying hens are crowded into small cages, so small that there is no room for all of the birds to sit down at once. They are given hormones to grow rapidly, and by the end of their lives they are so top heavy they can't stand up.

Another concern of factory farming is the **environmental impact**, including air pollution, water pollution, soil contamination, and erosion.

Air pollution is a by-product of factory farming. Most air pollution from farming comes in the form of carbon monoxide, carbon dioxide, and methane gas. Most food is grown away from urban areas; therefore, the food must be transported long distances, adding large amounts of carbon dioxide and carbon monoxide into the air. All livestock naturally produce methane.

The largest consumer of fuel in factory farming is chemical manufacturing, which also contributes to air pollution. As much as 40% of the energy used in the food system goes towards the production of chemical fertilizers and pesticides.[10]

Similarly, livestock production uses many natural resources and pollutes our air with methane. According to estimates by the United Nations Food and Agriculture Organization, 30% of the earth is involved in livestock production, with livestock generating nearly one fifth of the world's greenhouse gases, more than emissions from the transportation of agricultural products.[11]

Pesticide particles travel by the wind for many miles. Applying pesticides via aerial spraying is injurious to the health of farm workers and to those who live near factory farms. Burning crop residues instead of plowing or composting causes further air pollution.[12]

Water pollution is also a by-product of factory farming. The most common pollutants found in our water supplies are by-products of pesticide residues and runoff from synthetic fertilizers.[10] Animal waste is another contaminator. Animals that are raised in feedlots or cages deposit copious amounts of manure. The manure then must be collected and transported away from the area. This can be expensive. So to cut costs, it is sometimes dumped close to the feedlot, and, as a result, the surrounding soil becomes overloaded with contaminates causing ground and water pollution.[2]

Our oceans and lakes are also being polluted by fish farming (aquaculture). With the dramatic rise in human fish consumption, wild fish populations and many species are in danger of becoming extinct. To keep pace with the growing demand for fish, the fishing industry has created fish farms. These farms are located in oceans, lakes, and ponds, where fish are housed in enclosed areas and bred. These farms have introduced a new set of environmental problems. Some farms create excess waste that often seeps back into the oceans or lakes, destroying the natural habitat of wild fish. A farm with 200,000 salmon discharges more fecal waste than a city of 60,000 people.[9]

Soil contamination is mostly a by-product of fertilizers.[13] Factory farms often plant mono crops (crops replanted on the same plot of land), which use vast amounts of synthetic fertilizer; this practice encourages erosion.

These fertilizers have taken a toll on our topsoil, estimated at $40 billion per year, and contribute to the loss of micronutrients and minerals in fruits and vegetables.[13] Mono crops also reduce the types and varieties of crops grown. For example, in 1866, 1,186 varieties of fruits and vegetables were produced in California. Today, California's farms produce only 350 commercial crops.[14] Single-crop farms are more vulnerable to pests and require increasing amounts of synthetic pesticides, further harming the environment.

Another concern of large-scale factory farming is that it **compromises the local economy**. Large-scale factory farming tends to support other large corporate suppliers. Factory-farmed foods are generally found in nationwide grocery chains, and these national chains continue to displace locally owned businesses countrywide. *The San Francisco Retail Diversity Study* found that diverting just 10% of purchases from national chain stores to locally owned businesses would create 1,300 new jobs and yield nearly $200 million in incremental economic activity annually[15]. The study stated,

Local officials often fall for the seductions and political appeal of luring new national chains. They may even provide public funds or sales tax rebates for development. They're baited with promises of jobs and tax revenue, but they often fail to consider the greater losses that occur when the local business base is undermined. A chain may crow of creating 300 new jobs for a new big box store, but numerous studies indicate they displace more than one job for each (mostly lower-wage) job created.[15]

"Beginning in the early 1990s, millions of tons of sewage sludge have been applied to millions of acres of America's farmland as food crop fertilizer. Selling sewage sludge to farmers for use on cropland is a government program for disposing of the unwanted by-products from municipal wastewater treatment plants. The government has invented a gentler name for the sewage sludge: biosolids. Sewage sludge includes anything that is flushed, poured, or dumped into our nation's wastewater system—a vast, toxic mix of wastes collected from countless sources, from homes to chemical industries to hospitals. The sludge spread on our crop fields is a dangerous stew of heavy metals, industrial compounds, viruses, bacteria, drug residues, and radioactive material."[16]
Sewage sludge used in agriculture is regulated under the Clean Water Act.

Small-Scale Local Farming

Small-scale, locally owned farms usually utilize sustainable growing methods and raise their animals humanely, resulting in healthier food. These farmers are interested in preserving the land and investing in their local communities. Small-scale local farms, both conventional and organic, normally utilize crop rotations which maintain healthy soil, contributing to healthy crops and healthy yields. Small-scale farmers generally treat their animals well and respect the earth, which reduces environmental impact. Keeping business local supports and bolsters the local economy.

Animal welfare is closely tied to farm size. The smaller the farm, the better the living conditions for most animals. A growing number of farmers are starting smaller scale meat, poultry, dairy, and egg farms. These farmers have stopped feeding their animals grain, soy, and supplements meant to fatten the animals and have turned to the animals' native diets of natural grasses eaten during open-pasture grazing. As a result, these healthy animals grow at a natural pace in a low-stress environment as nature intended without the use of hormones, antibiotics, or other drugs.

Pollution emissions from small, local farms are much lower than from large-scale factory farms. Food that is grown locally doesn't have to travel long distances.

All **agricultural by-products** have the potential to enter our lakes, streams, rivers, and oceans. However, because organic and many smaller farms avoid both pesticides and synthetic fertilizers, their farming practices have a much better record in protecting water supplies from contamination.

Safe fish farming can be a great solution to the increasing pressures on our ocean resources. Half of our seafood comes from farms; people are raising fish, shrimp and oysters. But the ecological impact of fish farming depends on the species chosen, where the farm is located, and how they are raised.[17] Sustainable aquaculture limits habitat damage, prevents the spread of disease and non-native species, and minimizes the use of wild fish as feed.[18]

All farming, both organic and conventional, causes some level of soil degradation, decreasing soil fertility and contributing to soil erosion. But again, organic farmers don't use the harsh pesticides that conventional factory farmers use. Organic and small-farming-operation methods keep our soil healthier and reduce erosion. Fertility is maintained with compost and manure, which have been proven to increase levels of vitamins and minerals in produce.

Crop rotations keep the soil healthy, and encourage biodiversity. Most organic and small farmers tend to grow a wide variety of fruits and vegetables, both to protect biodiversity and to defend against infestations of pests forming on single crops.

Buying local gives those providers with local open space, including farms and pastures, an economic reason to keep the land open and undeveloped. Not only do small farms help the environment, but they also help our local economy. Supporting locally owned businesses means that we are reinvesting in our local economy and community. Research shows that local and independent businesses generate more than three times the return to our local economies than do national chain stores.[15]

Eating less meat will improve air quality. All livestock release methane as a bodily function. According to the Environmental Protection Agency, in the United States, "cattle emit about 5.5 million metric tons of methane per year into the atmosphere, accounting for 20% of U.S. methane emissions." Neither organic living conditions nor organic diets affect cows' methane emission levels.[19]

Local business owners typically purchase from other local businesses; therefore, these profits stay in our communities. Local businesses also offer the greatest opportunities for jobs, innovation, and other community contributions, which improve the quality of life for local residents.

Purchasing products from local purveyors is the most simple and effective way to address air, water, and soil pollution related to agriculture, whether it's organic or non-organic. The environmental benefits of local farming are simple: these businesses are located closer to home so their products require less transportation, thereby improving air quality by reducing emissions.

Local businesses give character to our communities. Owners of local businesses live in our neighborhoods, and their products and services support and sustain the needs of our residents. Local businesses play a vital role in our social networks and create a community with a sense of place and purpose.

Did you know?

- Hawaii imports 90% of its food.
- About 40% of our fruit is grown overseas.
- About one-third of all U.S. farms are located close to metropolitan areas, representing about 18% of total U.S. farmland.
- An American wheat farmer receives about six cents out of each dollar spent on a loaf of bread. This is about the cost of the packaging.
- Farmers markets enable farmers to keep 80 to 90 cents of each dollar spent by the consumer.
- Only 3.5 cents of each dollar spent in your typical grocery store actually goes to the farmer. If you buy food directly from farmers, you can be sure that most, if not all, of your money goes directly to them. When you purchase local at your co-op, over half your purchase goes to the farmer.[14]

1 Andrew, B., & Pirog, R. (2003). Checking the Food Odometer: Comparing Food Miles for Local Versus Conventional Produce Sales in Iowa Institutions. Retrieved December 10, 2009, from http://www.leopold.iastate.edu/research/marketing_files/foodmilespathways.html

2 Center for Urban Education and Sustainable Agriculture. (n.d.). Retrieved September 11, 2010, from http://www.cuesa.org/sustainable_ag/issues/cattle.php

3 Grass-Fed Basics. (n.d.). Retrieved December 1, 2009, from http://www.eatwild.com/basics.html

4 Broughton, K. S., Maiorano, G., Rule, D. C., & Shellito, S. M. (2002). Comparison of Muscle Fatty Acid Profiles and Cholesterol Concentrations of Bison, Beef Cattle, Elk, and Chicken. Journal of Animal Science, 80(5), 1202-11

5 Eat Local: Does your food travel more that you do? (n.d) Retrieved January 11, 2010, from http://www.nrdc.org/health/foodmiles

6 Heller, M. C., & Keoleian, G. A. (2000). Life Cycle-Based Stainability Indicators for Assessment of the U.S. Food System. Retrieved from The University of Michigan, Ann Arbor, Center for Sustainable Systems

7 The Humane Society. (n.d.). Retrieved September 11, 2010, from http://hsus.typepad.com/wayne/2009/09/epa-cafo-pollutants.html

8 Eat Wild, Grass-Fed Basics. (n.d.). Retrieved November 12, 2009, from http://www.eatwild.com/basics.html

9 It's all about salmon. Seafood Choices Alliance. (2005). Retrieved September 10, 2009, from http://www.seafoodchoices.com/resources/afishianado_pdfs/Salmon_Spring05.pdf

10 Fossil Fuel and Energy Use, (n.d.). Retrieved January 11, 2010, from http://www.sustainabletable.org/issues/energy

11 Bitman, Mark. (2009). Rethinking the Meat-Guzzler, The New York Times. Retrieved November 12, 2009, from http://www.nyt.com

12 Why eat organic? Nash Organic Produce. Retrieved December 1, 2009, from http://www.nashsorganicproduce.com/whyorganic.htm

13 Pimentel, David., & Pimentel, Marcia. (2004). Land, Water and Energy Versus The Ideal U.S. Population. Retrieved November 12, 2009, from http://www.npg.org/forum_series/forum0205.html

14 Eat Local, Be Local, What is Local? (n.d.). Retrieved January 1, 2010, from http://www.sustainabletable.org/issues/eatlocal/#didyouknow

15 Why Consumers Should Support Local Independent Businesses. (n.d.). Retrieved January 1, 2010, from http://www.organicconsumers.org/BTC/amiba041905.cfm

16 Nutrient Management and Fertilizer. (n.d.). Retrieved January 1, 2010, from http://www.epa.gov/oecaagct/tfer.html

17 Monterey Bay Aquarium Seafood Watch. (n.d.) Retrieved September 15, 2010, from www.montereybayaquarium.org/cr/cr_seafoodwatch/issues

18 Aquaculture, Ensuring That All is Well Down on the Fish Farm. (n.d.). Retrieved September 11, 2010, from http://www.montereybayaquarium.org/cr/cr_seafoodwatch/issues/aquaculture.aspx

19 Ruminant Livestock, Frequent Questions. (n.d.). Retrieved January 12, 2010, from http://www.epa.gov/rlep/faq.html

Healthy eating

Chapter two is a guide to understanding food labels – organic versus natural foods, organic certification tiers and the health benefits of eating foods from organic and small local farms. Pesticide levels in foods are reviewed as well as recommendations for healthy eating.

Organic fruits and vegetables are grown without the use of pesticides, synthetic fertilizers, sewage sludge, genetically modified organizisms (GMO), or ionizing radiation.[1] Organic meat, poultry, dairy, and eggs come from animals that were raised without antibiotics or growth hormones, are usually fed their native diet, and are sometimes allowed to roam freely.[1]

Not all natural and organic foods are the same. Our government has created an extensive organic certification program including many levels of certification, which can be confusing. More importantly there are many small local farmers who practice organic growing methods, but are often not certified Organic.

What Does the USDA Organic Seal Mean?

The USDA organic seal signifies to consumers the quality and integrity of organic products. Organic-certified operations must have an organic system plan and records that verify compliance with that plan. Operations are inspected randomly on an annual basis to ensure standards are being met.[1]

The USDA has created three labeling certification categories for organic products:

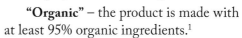

"100% Organic" – the product is made with 100% organic ingredients and displays the USDA Organic seal.[1]

"Organic" – the product is made with at least 95% organic ingredients.[1]

"Made With Organic Ingredients" – the product is made with a minimum of 70% organic ingredients with strict restrictions on the remaining 30%, including no GMOs.[1]

According to the United States Department of Agriculture (USDA), the "National Organic Program (NOP) defines organic as food that is produced by farmers who emphasize the use of renewable resources and the conservation of soil and water to enhance environmental quality for future generations. Organic meat, poultry, eggs, and dairy products come from animals that are given no antibiotics or growth hormones. Organic food is produced without using most conventional pesticides, fertilizers made with synthetic ingredients or sewage sludge, bioengineering, or ionizing radiation. Before a product can be labeled 'organic,' a government-approved certifier inspects the farm where the food is grown to make sure the farmer is following all the rules necessary to meet USDA organic standards. Companies that handle or process organic food before it gets to your local supermarket or restaurant must be certified, too."[1]

Products made with less than 70% organic ingredients may not make any organic claims on the front of the package, but may list organically produced ingredients on the side panel of the package.

Farmers who use organic practices but yield less than $5,000 worth of products annually are permitted to use the term "organic" without having their operations certified. However, these producers are prohibited from using the certified organic seal.[2]

Other Organic Food Labeling

Organic but not certified – Many farmers have chosen not to become certified for a variety of reasons. They cannot label their product *"Organic"*, so they use *"Organically Grown"*, *"Organic Methods"* or *"Organic, but not certified"*. If you are interested in a farmers product and certification is a concern, ask why they have chosen not to be certified.

Transitioning to Organic – Farmers need to practice organic production methods for three years before the products can be certified as "organic." *"Transitioning"* indicates that the farmland is going through a transition period, moving towards organic certification.

More Food Labeling

Note, many of these terms are not regulated or verified by a third party.

All natural or **Naturally grown** indicates that a product was processed and packaged without preservatives or additives, but it may include genetically modified ingredients or ingredients grown with pesticides. No federal regulatory body monitors natural foods. Natural products are not necessarily organic.

Biodynamic describes an organic production method that focuses on natural rhythms of the sun, moon, planets, and stars in an attempt to achieve harmony among people, plants, and animals. The Demeter Association believes "the farm as a living organism, self-contained and self-sustaining, responsible for creating and maintaining its individual health and vitality.[3] The NOP does not recognize the term "biodynamic" but the independent Demeter Association does certify that biodynamic products are organic.

Fair-trade indicates growers receive fair prices for their goods, grown in developing countries. For example, products might include coffee, tea, chocolate, and bananas.[4]

Free-range or **Cage-free** indicates that the animal was raised with access to the outdoors. The USDA only regulates this term for poultry. These regulations do not specify a minimum amount of outdoor time required for poultry to be labeled free-range. Free-range products are not necessarily organic.[4]

Raised without antibiotics indicates that livestock did not receive any antibiotics. Livestock raised without antibiotics is not necessarily organic.[4]

Grass-fed indicates that livestock was raised exclusively eating naturally on grasses and legumes. The American Grassfed Association is working on a certification program.[5]

Meadow-raised indicates that livestock was raised in a pasture on grasses and legumes but was also fed grains. Meadow-raised does not mean that the livestock is organic.[6]

No-hormones is a vague term. Hormones are commonly used in commercial farming to increase the rate of growth. Some of these hormones are natural, some are synthetic, and some are genetically engineered. Ask the farmers to explain if they use hormones and how.[6]

Vegetarian-fed indicates that livestock was not fed other animal parts.[6]

Certified Humane, American Humane Certified, or **Animal Welfare Approved** indicates that eggs came from chickens raised with care, not confined to battery cages or pumped with growth hormones or antibiotics. Not all humane claims are regulated.[4]

Muskegon Farmers Market – Muskegon, Michigan

More Facts About Organic Foods

Do organic foods cost more? Organic food isn't always more expensive, depending on where you shop. There are several reasons why the cost of organic food may be higher:

- Organic farmers don't receive federal subsidies as conventional farmers do; therefore, the price of organic food reflects the true cost of growing.[7]

- Organic farms are usually smaller than conventional farms and do not benefit from the economy of scale that larger growers enjoy.[7]

- Organic farming is more labor and management intensive.[7]

Is organic food more nutritious than conventional food? Various studies have yielded mixed results. "Research has shown that in some cases organic foods contain higher levels of naturally occurring chemical compounds including both health-promoting antioxidants and naturally occurring toxins that might impact human health."[8] However, it is extremely difficult to conduct studies due to many variables such as seeds, soil type, climate, postharvest handling, and crop variety that might affect nutrients.

Researchers at University of California, Davis performed a 10-year study "in which a specific strain of tomatoes was grown with pesticides on conventional soil next to the same strain grown on certified organic soil. All plants were subject to the same weather, irrigation, and harvesting conditions."[9] The results of the study found that organic tomatoes had more vitamin C and health-promoting antioxidants, more specifically flavonoids called kaempferol and quercetin. Researchers also noted that year-to-year nutrient content could vary in both conventional and organic plants.[9]

Other research shows the nutritional advantages of eating organic foods. According to The Organic Center, organic food is 25% higher in vitamin C and other antioxidants. Also, organically grown plants are 25% more nutrient dense, delivering more nutrients per calorie.[10]

Does organic food taste better? Taste is an individual matter, but a majority of chefs across the country choose to prepare local, seasonal, organic foods. Many argue that local, seasonal foods are better quality and have superior flavor than conventionally grown foods. Increasing numbers of consumers also believe organic food tastes better. It makes sense that well-tended, healthy plants and animals taste better.

Can washing and peeling your fruit and vegetables help remove pesticides? While washing and rinsing fresh produce may reduce levels of some pesticides, it does not completely eliminate them. Some fruits and vegetables tend to contain higher levels of contamination than others. Peeling reduces pesticide exposure, but valuable nutrients are lost removing the peel. The USDA found that, even after washing, certain types of produce carry higher levels of pesticide residue than others.[2]

Whenever possible, the best option is to choose foods from small, local farms; wash all produce; and eat a varied diet.

To reduce exposure to potentially harmful pesticides, choose organic foods instead of those from factory farms.

The nonprofit Environmental Working Group studied conventional fruits and vegetables and ranked them according to pesticide contamination. Visit page 10 for more information.

The nonprofit Environmental Working Group studied conventional fruits and vegetables and ranked them according to pesticide contamination.

Highest Pesticide Load

1	Peaches	100
2	Apples	96
3	Sweet Bell Peppers	86
4	Celery	85
5	Nectarines	84
6	Strawberries	83
7	Cherries	75
8	Lettuce	69
9	Grapes, Imported	68
10	Pears	65
11	Spinach	60
12	Potatoes	58
13	Carrots	57
14	Green Beans	55
15	Hot Peppers	53
16	Cucumbers	52
17	Raspberries	47
18	Plums	46
19	Oranges	46
20	Grapes Domestic	46
21	Cauliflower	39
22	Tangerines	38
23	Mushrooms	37
24	Cantaloupes	34
25	Lemons	31
26	Honeydew Melons	31
27	Grapefruits	31
28	Winter Squash	31
29	Tomatoes	30
30	Sweet Potatoes	30
31	Watermelons	25
32	Blueberries	24
33	Papayas	21
34	Eggplants	19
35	Broccoli	18
36	Cabbage	17
37	Bananas	16
38	Kiwis	14
39	Asparagus	11
40	Mangos	9
41	Pineapples	7
42	Avocados	1
43	Onions	1

Lowest Pesticide Load

Source: http://www.foodnews.org/walletguide.php

What's In Our Food?

Simply stated, crops need organic matter or fertilizer to flourish, and animals need food and shelter to mature. Better soil conditions create healthier crops, and better living conditions result in healthier animals; the outcome is a healthier product to eat. Learning what is in our food, and what is not in our food, along with the health benefits will allow you to make healthy decisions about the food you choose to consume.

Produce

Most issues relating to organic versus non-organic produce revolve around the use of pesticides. The majority of farming methods use pesticides when growing fruits and vegetables.

Some fruits and vegetables contain higher levels of contaminants than others, and some health experts believe that it is a good idea to eat organic versions of those fruits and vegetables that carry the highest pesticide loads.

The NOP allows natural (non-synthetic) substances and prohibits synthetic substances.[11] In addition, tests have shown that many types of produce pick up airborne pesticide residues from nearby farms.

Imported produce is more challenging to regulate. Increasing amounts of produce sold in the United States (both organic and non-organic) are imported from abroad.[11] It's easier to collect information about domestically grown produce, and even easier with locally grown produce.

In the United States, many foods are Genetically Modified (GM), and food companies aren't required to list GMs on their packaging. Most of the European Union requires GM labeling if GMs aren't banned.[12] The genetic modification of food involves removing genes from one species and placing them into another attempting to create more desirable traits. This could not only create modified species and new viruses, but also increase antibiotic resistance or alter the nutritional content of foods in detrimental ways. All organic food is made without GMs.[12]

Many food items from herbs and grains to potatoes and fruit are irradiated to kill insects, bacteria, mold, and microorganisms. Though the FDA permits irradiation, organic advocates claim that it would be unnecessary if producers simply kept cleaner food-processing facilities.[13]

Grains

Pesticide residues on conventional grain products, such as wheat and corn, tend to be low. However, conventional rice is grown with three times more pesticides than other grains. In addition, rice is grown in water, which carries more pesticide particles than soil.[14]

During storage, conventionally grown grain is treated with phosphine fumigants to kill insects that remain after harvesting. To reduce the likelihood of further insect growth, organic grain producers use carbon dioxide fumigants and ship their products more frequently.[14]

According to the USDA, approximately 70% of conventionally grown corn in the United States originates from genetically modified seeds.[14]

Cows and Dairy Products

A major benefit of pasture-raised animals is that their products are healthier for you. Butter made from the milk of grass-fed animals, whether organically raised or not, contains an essential omega-3 fatty acid called conjugated linolenic acid (CLA), which is missing from butter made from the milk of grain-fed cows.[15]

When it comes to dairy products, the size of the farm is often more important than its designation as organic or non-organic. Smaller farms tend to raise healthier animals, thereby increasing their productivity and reducing the need for antibiotics and hormones.[15] In fact, healthy cows produce more milk. On most small farms, organic or otherwise, animals are given more opportunities to graze in open pastures and have roomier barn accommodations than on industrial farms.[15]

The best way to ensure that you're consuming quality dairy products is to seek out products produced locally on small farms, organic or otherwise. These products compare very favorably with their organic counterparts, are safer, and will save you money. If the cost of organic dairy is prohibitive, you can find non-organic milk without rBGH. Look for terms like "rBGH-free" on labels.

Dairy and Soy Products

Learning what is in our dairy and soy products will allow you to make healthy decisions about the food you choose to consume.

Most milk purchased in the grocery store is pasteurized and homogenized. The pasteurization process involves heating the milk to 160°F for a few seconds and then cooling immediately. The high temperature kills any bacteria. Homogenization incorporates the milk so the fat and water don't separate. This involves shooting the milk through a fine nozzle to break-up the fat globules. As a result, the butterfat does not rise to the top.

Raw-milk is not pasteurized or homogenized, and is illegal to purchase in Michigan. However, if you choose to use raw-milk, you can buy into a herd-share at a local farm. There are no laws legalizing or prohibiting herd-shares. Raw milk cheese is available in Michigan and is required to be aged for 60 days as a precaution.

- **Pesticide residues:** Recent tests by the USDA have found only small amounts of pesticide residue in conventional whole milk samples. Conventional butter has been found to contain more residue, and organic butter contains less residue. But all butter is prone to picking up the airborne pesticide residue present in many environments.[16]

- **Antibiotic residues:** Although antibiotics are permitted for the treatment of cows with infected udders, the USDA tolerates no antibiotic residues in any milk samples. Milk found to contain traces of these residues is immediately discarded.[17]

- **Growth hormones:** BST otherwise known as rGBH has been administered to cows since the 1940s to increase milk production. In 1993, the FDA approved a synthetic version, rBST, for use. Milk from cows treated with hormones contains higher levels of a natural growth factor, and some experts believe there is a link between excess levels of rBST in humans and the likelihood of breast and prostate cancer. Also, studies suggest that adding hormones to the food supply disrupts the human endocrine system, and, as a result, boys and girls are developing at increasingly early ages.[18] Canada, Australia, New Zealand and most of Europe, by 2000 or earlier has banned growth hormones altogether.[18]

- **Pathogens:** Organic and non-organic milk are equally prone to bacterial contamination often caused by infected udders. To eliminate the chance of consuming a contaminated product, use pasteurized products.[18]

- **GMs:** Most non-organic cheeses are made with enzymes that are genetically engineered. Though organic regulations prohibit this practice, suppliers of organic enzymes are unreliable, and many experts doubt the authenticity claims made by producers of organic enzymes and cultures. Soy milk and cheese are made from soybeans; 85% of soy planted in the United States is genetically modified. Organic soybeans are required to be GM-free.[18]

Eggs and Chickens

Choosing chicken that is free-range and has been fed a vegetarian pastured diet has its health benefits. These chickens have three to six times more vitamin D in their eggs than in those of hens raised in

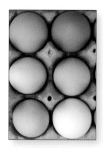

Earthscape Farm – Hesperia, Michigan

confinement.[19] Pastured hens are exposed to direct sunlight, which their bodies convert to vitamin D, which is passed on to their eggs. Vitamin D is best known for its role in building strong bones.[19] Recent research also shows that these eggs enhance the immune system, improve mood, reduce blood pressure, combat cancer, and reduce the risk of some autoimmune disorders.[19]

Mother Earth News collected samples from 14 pastured flocks across the country and had them tested at an accredited laboratory. The results were compared to official USDA data for commercial eggs. Results showed that the eggs from pastured flocks contained an amazing one-third less cholesterol than commercial eggs, one-fourth less saturated fat, two-thirds more vitamin A, two times more omega-3 fatty acids, and seven times more beta carotene.[19]

Most conventionally raised chickens used for both egg production and meat are housed in tiny, stacked cages within enormous factories that hold thousands of chickens.[20] Under these cramped conditions, chickens are prone to pecking or even killing one another, a problem that most conventional producers have solved by removing their beaks.[20] Some producers also practice forced molting, a practice where chickens are exposed to long periods of light and have their food withheld in order to shorten the period of time in which they naturally produce eggs. This practice forces chickens to lay eggs at a faster rate.[20]

Conventional producers often give their chickens a range of feed, whereas organic producers are prohibited from giving chickens feed which includes mammal protein. Organic chickens must be fed a wholly organic diet.

Organic producers are required to give chickens access to the outdoors, but this regulation does not stipulate a minimum amount of time, nor does it require any improved living conditions when chickens are not outdoors. Because the regulations are so vague, some producers include more specific labeling on their products. Free-run indicates the birds do not live in cages, free-range indicates the birds have access to the outdoors, and pastured birds live outside in fenced enclosures.

Meat

The issue of organic versus non-organic meat is most closely tied to animal welfare issues, although there are also health considerations. For example, meat from grass-fed cattle, bison, lambs, pigs, and goats has less total fat, saturated fat, cholesterol, and calories.[15] It also has more vitamin E, beta-carotene, vitamin C, and a number of health-promoting

fats, including omega-3 fatty acids.[15] Other important facts are as follows:

- **Livestock disease:** Farmers have fed livestock corn and soybeans for decades because these foods encourage rapid weight gain.[7] Many cows were also fed rendered animal parts (dehydrated bits of animals) until 1997, when it was found that this additive may have contributed to the outbreak of mad cow disease.[21] Some conventional livestock producers feed their cows poultry manure, and some studies suggest this may increase rates of Crohn's disease in humans.[21] Organic regulations prohibit the use of both rendered animal parts and manure in livestock feed and require that all animals be fed a wholly organic diet.

- **Pesticide residues:** Most livestock eat a conventionally grown corn and soybean diet (organic livestock eat an organic-only diet).[22] The USDA has found little evidence of pesticide residues in beef samples. All beef products are equally susceptible to pick up airborne residues.

- **Antibiotics:** Conventional beef cattle are often given antibiotics to prevent illness and stimulate growth. Antibiotic residues in meat products are harmful to humans, as antibiotics encourage the development of drug-resistant strains of bacteria that may be transmitted to humans.[23]

- **Hormones:** The USDA permits the use of hormones in beef cattle to promote growth and reduce feed requirements. The use of growth hormones is prohibited in organic beef cattle.[22]

- **Parasiticides:** Cattle conventionally raised are given synthetic parasiticides to control parasite growth. Organic producers normally treat their cattle with nonsynthetic alternatives.[22]

- **Pathogens:** All meat is susceptible to the growth of food-borne bacteria. Meat products are most vulnerable to these pathogens when they are stored improperly or processed in unsanitary facilities.[24]

Earthscape Farm – Hesperia, Michigan

Seafood and Fish

Seafood plays a important role in a healthy diet. It's an excellent source of protein, low in saturated fat, and a good source of omega-3 fatty acids, which benefit the heart and reduce the risk of stroke as well as other health issues.[25] And omega-3's are important from the womb to tomb, according to the U.S. Food and Drug Administration. Studies indicate that mothers who ate fish during their last trimester increased the duration of gestation therefore increasing birth weight.[31]

The American Heart Association recommends eating fish at least twice a week.[25] But some fish can be unhealthy if consumed frequently because they contain high levels of environmental contaminants. Mercury levels are generally highest in older, larger, predatory fish and marine mammals.

Some types of farmed fish are healthier than there wild counterparts according to the Environmental Defense Fund Seafood Selector.[25] Recommendations for eating farmed fish include; Arctic char, clams, mussels, oysters, striped bass, and rainbow trout.

In the United States, fish can't be certified as organic. The USDA has not yet issued regulations on organic seafood.

To purchase clean, healthy fish, find a reputable fish monger. They most often know the source of their fish, as well as fishing methods utilized. When you buy seafood, ask where your seafood comes from and whether it is farmed or wild-caught. When purchasing seafood, keep in mind that domestic seafood contaminants are more easily traced. To support healthy oceans and lakes, purchase fish caught or farmed using environmentally friendly practices.

Michigan's Fresh Water Fish

Michigan has many consumable wild fish species including herring, rainbow smelt, salmon, trout, whitefish, walleye, and yellow perch. Local fish can be found at small fish markets around the state and are sold fresh, frozen or smoked.

Whitefish contains more omega-3 fatty acids than pink and sockeye salmon. EPA and DHA, which are found in high levels in Great Lakes whitefish are essential in the development of the human fetus, and critical in human brain development and retinal tissue.[31]

Great Lakes Whitefish are rigorously monitored for contaminants and pass FDA standards for consumption. Lake whitefish as a species, are at the bottom of the scale in mercury buildup as well.[31] Lab tests have verified that fish from the Great Lakes have minimal contaminates and fall well below the FDA's trigger points for safe consumption.[32]

To learn more about fresh water fish from the Great Lakes visit the Michigan Sea Grant website at miseagrant.umich.edu, and Great Lakes Whitefish at greatlakeswhitefish.com.

Muskegon Farmers Market – Muskegon, Michigan

Historic Fishtown – Leland, Michigan

Purchasing Recommendations

Many consumers balance their health concerns with a limited food budget. The following lists include the health benefits and budgetary concerns of healthy shopping.

Health Benefits

- Organic fruits and vegetables may have more nutritional value and expose you to less pesticides. To reduce pesticide exposure by almost 90%, try organic produce for the top 12 most contaminated fruits and vegetables (peaches, apples, sweet bell peppers, celery, nectarines, strawberries, cherries, lettuce, imported grapes, pears, spinach, and potatoes).[8]

- Eggs from pasture-raised hens have three to six times more vitamin D.[19]

- Organic or pasture-fed chicken has a higher amount of omega-3 fatty acids and vitamin A.[15]

- Grass-fed cows have more antioxidants, omega 3, CLA, and vitamins.[15]

- Grass-fed cattle, bison, lamb, pig, and goat products have less total fat, saturated fat, cholesterol, and calories. They also have more vitamin E, beta-carotene, vitamin C, and a number of health-promoting fats, including omega-3 fatty acids.[15]

- Michigan whitefish is an excellent source of omega-3 fatty acids, which benefit the heart and EPA and DHA which benefit critical human brain development and retinal tissue.[31] .

Gregory Camp – on the Tahquamenon

Budgetary Concerns

There are many options for purchasing fresh organic foods that are reasonably priced in our community. There may be no single source for organic foods at the right price, so become creative.

- Shop at farmers markets. They are a great source for fresh local and organic foods.

- Buy in bulk and seconds (blemished produce) for the best discounts.

- Buy a share in a CSA (community supported agriculture program). In return, you will receive weekly boxes of fresh fruits and vegetables from the upcoming harvest.

- Join a food co-op, a member-owned business that provides groceries and other products to its members at a discount. Many of the products lining the shelves of co-ops are organic, and much of the produce comes from local family farms.

- Buy in season. The absolute best time to buy organic fruits or vegetables is at the peak of ripeness, when these foods are abundant and cheaper. Freeze and can the extras.

- Buy preserved foods during the off season, such as frozen or dried organic fruits and vegetables. They often have better flavor than imported winter foods.

- Embrace the freezer. Freeze your fresh fruits and vegetables, and use them in the winter as treats.

- Grow your own produce by starting a garden.

- Buy organic produce with the smallest price difference between organic and non-organic varieties including broccoli, cabbage, carrots, celery, potatoes, radishes, and turnips.

- Buy dairy products from smaller local farms; the farm size is often more important than its designation as organic or non-organic. Small farm products compare favorably with their organic counterparts and should save you money.

Industrial Farming is Giving us Less Nutritious Food

The commercially grown vegetables, fruits and grains that we are eating today are significantly less nutritious than these foods were 100 years ago, or even just 30 years ago.

- In wheat and barley, protein concentrations declined by 30 to 50 percent between the years 1938 and 1990.
- Likewise, a study of 45 corn varieties developed from 1920 to 2001, grown side by side, found that the concentrations of protein, oil and three amino acids have all declined in the newer varieties.
- Six minerals have declined by 22 to 39 percent in 14 widely grown wheat varieties developed over the past 100 years.
- Official U.S. Department of Agriculture (USDA) nutrient data shows that the calcium content of broccoli averaged 12.9 milligrams per gram of dry weight in 1950, but only 4.4 mg/g dry weight in 2003.

All of this evidence has been assembled and rigorously reviewed by Dr. Donald R. Davis, a now (mostly) retired chemist from the University of Texas.

So what's causing these declines? The evidence indicates there are at least two forces at work. The first is what agriculture researchers call the environmental "dilution effect." Davis notes that researchers have known since the 1940s that yield increases produced by fertilization, irrigation and other environmental means used in industrial farming tend to decrease the concentrations of minerals in those plants. These techniques give growers higher yields, and consumers get less expensive food. But now it appears there's a hidden long-term cost—lowered food quality.

For example, a study of phosphorous fertilizer on raspberries found that applying high levels of phosphorus caused the yield to double and concentrations of phosphorus to increase in the plants, but meanwhile levels of eight other minerals declined by 20 to 55 percent!

The other force at work is what Davis calls the *genetic* dilution effect—the decline in nutrient concentration that results when plant breeders develop high-yielding varieties without a primary focus on broad nutrient content. That's what the studies of wheat, corn and broccoli confirm.

In fruits, vegetables and grains, usually 80 to 90 percent of the dry weight yield is carbohydrates—sugars and starches (the last things we need more of in the American diet). Davis says that when breeders (and growers) specifically choose varieties for high yields, they are selecting mostly for the highest amounts of carbohydrates.

"These studies suggest to me that genetic dilution effects may be common when selective breeding successfully increases crop yield," Davis says. USDA data indicate that yields have increased an average of 1.8 fold for 24 vegetables and 1.3 fold for six fruits over the past 30 years.

What can we do? Vegetables and fruits are our richest sources of many vitamins and minerals. It seems likely that those of us who grow food gardens (or shop at farmers markets) will get more nutrient-dense foods if we grow (or pay a premium for) older, lower-yielding heirloom varieties. Odds are good that heirloom varieties may be more nutritious than current supermarket fare. Plus, using organic methods such as moderate amounts of slow-release fertilizers should help us get maximum nutrition from our homegrown produce. And most important of all, Davis points out that the nutrient declines in *processed* foods are much deeper and broader than the declines in fresh, whole foods.

From MOTHER EARTH NEWS[10] by Cheryl Long: Reprinted with permission from Mother Earth News. Copyright 2009.

MONTEREY BAY AQUARIUM SEAFOOD WATCH
A Consumers Guide to Sustainable Seafood

Seafood Central U.S. *Seafood may appear in more than one column*

Best Choices	Good Alternatives	Avoid
Arctic Char (farmed)	Caviar, Sturgeon (US farmed)	Caviar, Sturgeon* (imported wild)
Barramundi (US farmed)	Clams, Oysters (wild)	Chilean Seabass/Toothfish*
Catfish (US farmed)	Cod: Pacific (US trawled)	Cod: Atlantic, imported Pacific
Clams (farmed)	Crab: Blue*, King (US), Snow	Crab: King (imported)
Cod: Pacific (Alaska longline)	Flounder, Sole (Pacific)	Flounder, Halibut, Sole (Atlantic)
Crab: Dungeness, Stone	Herring: Atlantic, Lake	Grouper*
Halibut: Pacific	Lobster: American/Maine	Lobster: Spiny (Brazil)
Lobster: Spiny (US)	Mahi Mahi/Dolphinfish (US)	Mahi Mahi/Dolphinfish (imported)
Mussels (farmed)	Pollock (Alaska wild)	Monkfish
Oysters (farmed)	Scallops: Sea	Orange Roughy*
Salmon (Alaska wild)	Shrimp (US, Canada)	Rockfish (Pacific trawled)
Scallops (farmed off-bottom)	Squid	Salmon (farmed, including Atlantic)*
Striped Bass (farmed or wild*)	Swai, Basa (farmed)	Shark*
Tilapia (US farmed)	Swordfish (US)*	Shrimp (imported)
Trout: Rainbow (farmed)	Tilapia (Central America farmed)	Snapper: Red
Tuna: Apoundacore including canned	Tuna: Bigeye, Yellowfin (troll/pole)	Swordfish (imported)*
white tuna (troll/pole, US and BC)	Tuna: Canned white/Apoundacore	Tilapia (Asia farmed)
Tuna: Skipjack including canned	(troll/pole except US and BC)	Tuna (longline)*
light tuna (troll/pole)		Tuna: Bluefin* and Tongol
		Yellowtail (imported farmed)

Sushi *Seafood may appear in more than one column*

Best Choices	Good Alternatives	Avoid
Amaebi/Spot Prawn (BC)	Amaebi/Spot Prawn (US)	Ankimo/Monkfish Liver
Awabi/Abalone (US farmed)	Ebi/Shrimp (US, Canada)	Ankoh/Monkfish
Gindara/Sablefish/Black Cod (AK, BC)	Gindara/Sablefish/Black Cod	Ebi/Shrimp (imported)
Ikura/Salmon roe (AK wild)	(CA, OR or WA)	Hamachi/Hiramasa/Yellowtail
Iwana/Arctic Char (farmed)	Hirame/Karei/Flounder,	(imported, farmed)
Iwashi/Pacific Sardines (US)	Sole (Pacific)	Hirame/Karei/Flounder, Sole,
Izumidai/Tilapia (US farmed)	Hotate/Sea Scallops	Halibut (Atlantic)
Kaki/Oysters (farmed)	Izumidai/Tilapia (Central America	Hon Maguro/Bluefin Tuna*
Kani/Crab: Dungeness, Stone	farmed)	Izumidai/Tilapia (Asia farmed)
Katsuo/Bonito/Skipjack Tuna	Kani/Crab: Blue*, King (US), Snow	Kani/Crab: King (imported)
(troll/pole)	Kanikama/Surimi/Pollock (AK)	Maguro/Tuna: Bigeye*, Yellowfin*
Masago/Smelt Roe (Iceland)	Maguro/Tuna: Bigeye, Yellowfin	Sake/Salmon (CA, OR* wild)
Mirugai/Giant Clam/Geoduck (wild)	(troll/pole)	Sake/Salmon (farmed, including
Muurugai/Mussels (farmed)	Masago/Smelt Roe (Canada)	Atlantic)*
Sake/Salmon (AK wild)	Sake/Salmon (WA wild)*	Shiro Maguro/Apoundacore Tuna*
Sawara/Spanish Mackerel (US)*	Shiro Maguro/Apoundacore Tuna	(imported)
Shiro Maguro/Apoundacore Tuna	(Hawaii)*	Tai/Red Snapper
(troll/pole, BC and US)	Squid	Tako/Octopus
Suzuki/Striped Bass (farmed or wild*)	Tai/Red Porgy (US)	Toro/Tuna: Bigeye*, Bluefin*,
Uni/Sea Urchin Roe (Canada)	Toro/Tuna: Bigeye, Yellowfin	Yellowfin*
	(troll/pole)	Unagi/Freshwater Eel (farmed)
	Uni/Sea Urchin Roe (CA)	Uni/Sea Urchin Roe (Maine)

Key

Best Choices Abundant, well-managed, and caught or farmed in environmentally friendly ways.	Good Alternatives Some concerns with how fish are caught, farmed, or the health of their habitat due to human impact.	Avoid Overfished, caught or farmed in ways that harm marine life or the environment.
BC = British Columbia CA = California	OR = Oregon WA = Washington	*Limit consumption due to concerns about contaminants.

These recommendations are researched by Monterey Bay Aquarium. The Monterey Bay Aquarium Seafood Watch program creates science-based recommendations that help consumers and businesses make ocean-friendly seafood choices.

1 National Organic Program. Organic Foods Production Act of 1990. (2005) Retrieved November 1, 2009, from http://www.ams.usda.gov

2 Gold, M. V. (2009). USDA National Agricultural Library, Organic Production & Organic Food. Retrieved November 2, 2009, from http://www.nal.usda.gov/afsic/pubs/ofp/ofp.shtml

3 Demeter Biodynamic Farming. (n.d.). Retrieved September 20, 2010, from http://www.demeter-usa.org

4 Rickard, Wendy. Making Sense of Food Labels. (n.d.). Retrieved September 10, 2010, from http://life.gaiam.com/gaiam/p/Making-Sense-of-Food-Labels.html

5 Standards American Grass-deed Association. (n.d.) Retrieved September 1, 2010, from http://www.americangrassfed.org/our-standards-and-certification

6 Grass-Fed Basics. (n.d.). Retrieved December 1, 2009, from http://www.eatwild.com/basics.html

7 Organic 101, The Organic Center. (n.d.) Retrieved September 1, 2010, from http://www.organic-center.org/organic101.html

8 Winter, C. (2007). Consumers Face Trade-offs in Choosing Organic or Conventional Foods. Retrieved from The University of California, Davis Web Site: http://caes.ucdavis.edu/NewsEvents/web-news/2007/02/consumers-face-trade-offs-in-choosing-organic-or-conventional-foods

9 Foreman, J. (2008). Comparing Apples to Organic Apples. *The Boston Globe*. Retrieved November 1, 2009, from http://www.boston.com

10 Andrews, P., Davies, N., Yana, J., & Zhao, X. (2008). New Evidence Confirms the Nutritional Superiority of Plant-based Organic Foods. Retrieved from http://www.organic-center.org/news.pr.php?action=detail &pressrelease_id=22

11 Principles of Organic Farming. (n.d.). Retrieved September 20, 2010, from http://www.sarep.ucdavis.edu/organic/complianceguide/faq.htm

12 Estabrook, Barry. (2010). Feds on GMO Labeling: Don't Tell, Don't Ask. Retrieved September 20, 2010 from http://www.theatlantic.com/food/archive/2010/04/feds-on-gmo-labeling-dont-tell-dont-ask/39452/

13 FDA (Food and Drug Administration). Pesticide Residue Monitoring Program Results and Discussion FY 2006. Food and Drug Administration. June 1, 2008.

14 (2010) Adoption of Genetically Engineered Crops in the U.S. Retrieved August 30, 2010, from http://www.ers.usda.gov/Data/BiotechCrops

15 Health Benefits of Grass-Fed Products. Retrieved August 20, 2009, from http://www.eatwild.com/healthbenefits.htm

16 Andrews, Dominique. Buying organic food on a budget. (n.d.). Retrieved August 29, 2009, from http://www.kgun9.com/Global/story.asp?S=11785528

17 Sustainable Table the Issues Pesticides. Retrieved August 29, 2009, from http://www.sustainabletable.org/issues/pesticides

18 (2008). Consumers Drive Hormone-free Milk. *The Grand Rapids Press*. Retrieved November 1, 2009, from http://blog.mlive.com

19 Alderman, T., & Long, C. (2007). Meet Real Free-Range Eggs. *Mother Earth News*. Retrieved from http://www.motherearthnews.com/Real-Food/2007-10-01/Tests-Reveal-Healthier-Eggs.aspx

20 Fanatico, Anne. Poultry Production in the U.S. (2008). Retrieved September 20, 2010, from http://www.attra.ncat.org/attra-pub/organicpoultry.html

21 Daniel, J. & Olson, K. (2005). Feeding Poultry Litter to Beef Cattle. Retrieved from The University of Missouri, http://extension.missouri.edu/publications/DisplayPub.aspx?P=G2077

22 Pasture-Based Farming Enhances Animal Welfare. Retrieved August 20, 2009, from http://eatwild.com/animals.html

23 (2003). Most Consumers Unaware of Antibiotic Residues in Meat. Retrieved from http://www.organicconsumers.org/foodsafety/beef052903.cfm

24 Grass-Fed Products are Clean and Safe. Retrieved August 20, 2009, from http://eatwild.com/foodsafety.html

25 American Heart Association. Fish 101. Retrieved August 23, 2010, from http://americanheart.org/presenter.jhtml?identifier=3071550

26 Superfish A Warning to Seafood Lovers. Retrieved July 20, 2010, from http://www.pbs.org/wnet/nature/episodes/superfish/a-warning-to-seafood-lovers/1008

27 (2010). Make Smart Choices When Eating Seafood. Environmental Defense Funds Seafood Selector. http://www.edf.org/page.cfm?tagID=1521

28 (2008). Impacts of Fishing and Results of Sustainable Fish Policies. Retrieved September 15, 2010, from http://innovation.edf.org/page.cfm?tagID=30957

29 A Look at the Biggest Challenges—And the Way Forward. Retrieved September 15, 2010, from http://montereybayaquarium.org/cr/cr_seafoodwatch/issues

30 Long, C. (2009). Industrial Farming is giving us Less Nutritious Food. *Mother Earth News*. Retrieved from www.motherearthnews.com/Sustainable-Farming/Nutrient-Decline-Industrial-Farming.aspx

31 Great Lakes Whitefish, Eating Fish: Science Says–Health Benefits of Eating Whitefish. Retrieved May 2, 2011, from www.greatlakeswhitefish.com.

32 Fish Contaminant Monitoring Program Data Summary for Lakes Superior, Huron, and Michigan, Inter-Tribal Fisheries and Assessment Program. 2008.

Wild Blueberries – Seney, Michigan

Blackbird Gardens – Petoskey, Michigan

Muskegon Farmers Market – Muskegon, Michigan

Michigan's crops

Chapter three details Michigan's agriculture, where to purchase local fresh foods and the time of year each crop reaches its seasonal peak.

Fresh local foods are taking their place at our tables. Michigan has an abundance of fruit and vegetable crops, as well as meat, poultry, fish and dairy. Fresh produce is widely available during the summer and fall months. Meat, poultry, and dairy, can be found year-round. Purchase these high-quality, local foods at farmers markets, pick your produce at your neighborhood community garden, become a member in a community supported agriculture (CSA) program, or join a local cooperative grocery store.

Farmers markets offer fresh products and attract people from all walks of life, thereby bringing families and communities together. According to the Michigan Farmers Market Association (MIFMA) in 2010, there were 220 farmers markets throughout the state. These markets operate several days per week, providing customers with easy, frequent access to fresh local foods. Farmers markets also give you the opportunity to speak directly with the farmer, allowing you to learn more about the crops, growing practices, and upcoming crop varieties. Many small farmers employ farming practices just as rigorous as those required of certified organic farms, but because of expense, they do not seek certification.

Community gardens are a great way to actively participate in growing your own food. They are found throughout the state and are gaining in popularity. A community garden is a piece of land gardened by a group of people. The American Community Gardening Association (ACGA) "has a broad definition of what a community garden entails. It can be urban, suburban, or rural. It can grow flowers or vegetables."[1] It can be one community plot, or many individual plots. It can be at a school, hospital, or in a neighborhood.[1] Members of a community garden share the expense, share the labor, and share the harvest. Produce is normally grown for the members and contributors of the garden, but it also can be sold for profit for an organization such as a church or school.

Community supported agriculture (CSA) allows consumers to buy local, seasonal food directly from the farmer – a great way to enjoy a bountiful harvest of local seasonal produce. Members generally pay "a share" to the farmer at the beginning of the harvest season and, in return, receive a box of produce once or twice per week for the duration of that season. Your box will differ from week to week depending upon the seasonal crops planted. Some CSAs not only provide produce but also offer fresh meat, poultry, dairy, and cheese. According to Local Harvest, there are over 180 CSAs in the state.[2]

Cooperative grocers (co-ops) are also a great local shopping resource. Most co-ops require a small monthly fee or work for trade to become a member. They are dedicated to buying high quality natural and organic groceries from socially conscious companies. Co-ops also carry a large selection of artisan foods, local dairy and fair-trade products, as well as organic bulk dry goods such as flour, nuts and spices. Co-ops may have lower prices on comparable products than your supermarket. According to the Natural Cooperative Grocers Association, there are eight co-ops in the state. Buying clubs have similar products to a co-op but without a store front.[3]

Crops By Season

Michigan crops are at peak ripeness during the spring, summer, and fall months. To assist you in creating the recipes in this book, the following charts detail when crops are at their peak ripeness. A comprehensive listing of local resources can be found on our website under the references link at www.michigansguidetolocalcooking.com.

Vegetables	Jan	Feb	Mar	Apr	May	June	July	Aug	Sept	Oct	Nov	Dec
Arugula	•	•	•	•	•	•			•	•	•	•
Asparagus					•	•						
Beans, Green or Wax						•	••	•	••			
Beets	•	•	•	•	•	••	•	•	•	•	•	•
Bok choy						•			•			
Broccoli						•	•	•	•	•	•	
Brussel Sprouts										•	•	
Cabbage							•	•	•	•	•	
Carrots							•	•	•	•	•	•
Cauliflower							•	•	•	•		
Celery							•	•	•	•	•	
Chard	•	•	•	•	•	••	•	•	•	••	•	•
Corn							•	•	•			
Cucumbers						•	••	•	•			
Eggplant							••			•		
Greens-Asian (Minzuna, Pac Choi, Tatsoi, etc)	•	•	•	•	••	•			•	•	•	•
Greens-Cooking (Beet, Collard, Mustard, Turnip)	•	•	•	•	••	•	•					
Fennel							•		•	•		
Kale	•	•	•	•	•	••	•	•	•	•	•	•
Kohlrabi						•	•	•	•	•		
Leeks					•				•	•	•	
Lettuce (Bibb, Iceberg, Leaf, Romaine)					•	•	•	•	•	•	•	•
Mushrooms								•	•	•		
Onions								•	•	•		

source: Putting Michigan Produce on Your Menu[4]

• field fresh   • extended growing season

Many farmer's are utilizing hoop-houses to extend their growing seasons. Hoop-houses protect crops from the inclement weather. A hoop-house is similar to a green house but is not a permanent structure and is cheaper to build. Unlike a greenhouse, a hoop-house does not have a ventilation or a heating system, and uses passive solar energy to warm the plants. For cooling, the hoop-house has adjustable side panels that roll up for cross-ventilation.

Vegetables	Jan	Feb	Mar	Apr	May	June	July	Aug	Sept	Oct	Nov	Dec
Parsnips				•	•				•	•		
Peas						•			•	•		
Peppers						•	• •	•	•	•	•	
Potatoes								•	•	•	•	
Pumpkins									•	•	•	
Radishes	•	•	•	• •	•	•	•	•	•	•	•	•
Rutabagas									•	•	•	
Salad Greens	•	•	•	•	•			•	•	•		•
Spinach	•	•	•	•	•	• •	•		•		• •	•
Squash, summer						•	• •	•	• •	•		
Squash, winter									•	•		
Tomatoes							•	•	•			
Turnips					•	•			•	•		
Zucchini							•	•	•			

Fruit	Jan	Feb	Mar	Apr	May	June	July	Aug	Sept	Oct	Nov	Dec
Apples							•	•	•	•		
Apricots							•	•				
Blueberries							•		•			
Blackberries								•	•			
Cantaloupes							• •	•	•			
Cherries, Sweet						•	•	•				
Cherries, Tart							•	•				
Cranberries									•	•		
Grapes									•	•	•	
Nectarines								•	•			
Peaches							•	•	•			
Pears								•	•	•		
Plums								•	•			
Raspberries							•	•	•	•		
Rhubarb					•							
Strawberries						•	• •	•	•	•		
Watermelons								•	•			

source: Putting Michigan Produce on Your Menu[4]

• field fresh • extended growing season

Crops By Season

Herbs	Jan	Feb	Mar	Apr	May	June	July	Aug	Sept	Oct	Nov	Dec
Basil	•	•	•	•	•	•	•	•	•	•	•	•
Chives	•	•	•	•	•	•	••	•	•	•	•	•
Cilantro	•	•	•	•	•	•	•	••	•	•	•	•
Dill	•	•	•	•	•	•	•	•	•	•	•	•
Garlic							•	•				
Mint	•	•	•	•	•	•	•	•	•	•	•	•
Oregano	•	•	•	•	•	•	•	•	•	•	•	•
Parsley	•	•	•	•	•	••	•	•	•	••	•	•
Rosemary	•	•	•	•	•	•	••	•	•	••	•	•
Sage	•	•	•	•	•	•	•	•	•	•	••	•
Thyme	•	•	•	•	•	•	•	•	•	•	••	•

source: *Putting Michigan Produce on Your Menu*[4]

Others	Jan	Feb	Mar	Apr	May	June	July	Aug	Sept	Oct	Nov	Dec
Chestnuts										•	•	•
Dry Beans								•	•	•		
Honey						•	•	•	•	•		
Maple Syrup		•	•	•								

source: *Michigan Specialty Crops*[5]

• field fresh • extended growing season

Other Specialty Foods

Chestnuts – Michigan chestnuts are sold fresh, frozen, peeled, sliced, or as flour. Chestnut flour is a gluten-free alternative to wheat flour. Peeled, frozen, and dehydrated, chestnuts are available year-round.[5]

Dry Edible Beans – Michigan producers grow several classes of dry edible beans, including: Azuki Beans, Black Beans, Cranberry Beans, Great Northern Beans, Red Kidney Beans, Navy Beans, Pinto Beans, Small Red Beans, and Yellow Eye Beans.[5]

Honey – Producers across Michigan gathered a total of 5 million pounds of honey in 2008, ranking Michigan seventh in the nation in honey production. Raw honey has more nutrients than heated, filtered honey.[5]

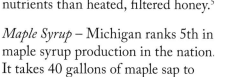

Maple Syrup – Michigan ranks 5th in maple syrup production in the nation. It takes 40 gallons of maple sap to make one gallon of maple syrup.[5]

Michigan's Top 10 Agricultural Facts

1. Michigan is the nation's leading producer of blueberries, tart red cherries, cucumbers (grown for pickles), Niagara grapes, potatoes (grown for potato chips), squash, as well as dry beans such as black, cranberry, light red, and kidney.[6]

2. Michigan is one of the nation's leading producers of traditional crops such as corn, wheat, and soybeans.[6]

3. Michigan is the second most agriculturally diverse state in the country; California is first. Michigan's unique micro-climates allow farmers to grow over 200 different types of food products.[6]

4. Michigan is the nation's second largest producer of all dry beans, celery, and carrots. The U.S. Senate is required to serve bean soup daily, which includes Michigan white beans.[6]

5. Michigan is the nation's third largest producer of apples and asparagus.

6. Michigan is the nation's fourth largest producer of grapes, and eighth in the nation for wine grape production.[7]

7. Michigan ranks in the top five in the nation in the production of all dry beans, celery, apples, asparagus, snap beans, carrots, Concord grapes, radishes, sweet cherries, plums, sugar beets, tomatoes, and pumpkins.[6]

8. Michigan ranks sixth in the nation for the number of breweries, microbreweries, and brewpubs, supporting its claim as "The Great Beer State."[8]

9. Michigan's agriculture industry contributes more than $71 billion annually to the state's economy. It's the second largest industry in the state, the auto industry being first.[6]

10. Michigan is home to about 10 million acres of farmland and about 56,000 farms. Over ninety percent of these are family-owned farms, many of which have been in the same family for generations.[6]

L. Mawby Vineyard – Lelanau Peninsula

Michigan Wine

Michigan has about 14,000 acres of vineyards. About 2,000 acres are devoted to wine grapes, making it eighth in nation for wine grape production. In fact, vineyard area has increased more than 60% in the last 10 years.[7]

Michigan's 73 commercial wineries produce more than 1 million gallons of wine annually, ranking 13th in the nation for wine production. The vast majority of production is from Michigan-grown grapes.[7]

Three types of grapes are used for Michigan wines: Vinifera, Hybrid, and Native. Most of Michigan's quality wine grapes grow within 25 miles of Lake Michigan.

Harvest begins for early varieties at the end of August in the southwest and may extend into November for late-ripening vinifera varieties in the northwest.[7]

Increasingly, Michigan wines are receiving high honors at national and international competitions. In addition, the Michigan Wine and Spirits Competition provides for head-to-head comparisons of the best Michigan wines.[7] Following each year's competition, results are posted at michiganwines.com.

Michigan wineries make many styles of wine, from dry to sweet, including ice wine, sparkling, fortified, fruit wines, and eau-de-vie (fruit brandy). Michigan wines are typically "cool climate": clean, crisp, balanced wines that exhibit true varietal character.[7]

Besides grape wine, Michigan is a leader in the production of fruit wines such as cherry wine.

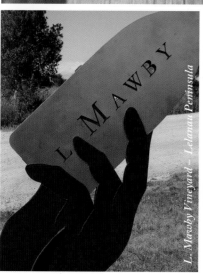

L. Mawby Vineyard – Lelanau Peninsula

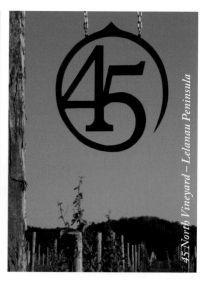

45 North Vineyard – Lelanau Peninsula

Michigan Microbrew

Our Great Lakes state should also be known as "The Great Beer State," according to the Michigan Brewers Guild. Michigan ranks sixth in the nation for the number of breweries, microbreweries, and brew pubs. Presently, there are more than 70 craft breweries in the state."[8] Crafty brewers have also created a seasonal bright red cherry ale, using only Michigan cherries.

Michigan's thriving brewing industry contributes over $24 million in wages with a total economic contribution of more than $133 million.[8]

©fotolinchen

[1] *What is a Community Garden?* American Community Garden Association. (n.d.). Retrieved August 20, 2010, from http://www.communitygarden.org/learn

[2] CSA's Michigan Local Harvest. (n.d.). Retrieved August 20, 2010, from http://www.localharvest.org/search-csa.jsp?st=24&ty=6&nm=

[3] National Cooperative Grocers Association. Michigan Locations. (n.d.). Retrieved August 1, 2010, from http://www.ncga.coop/stores

[4] *Putting Michigan Produce on Your Menu.* C.S. Mott Group for Sustainable Food Systems at Michigan State University.

[5] *Michigan Specialty Crops.* Michigan Department of Agriculture. Retrieved June 10, 2010, from http://www.michigan.gov/documents/mda/MDA_Crops_Brochure_low-resolution_324586_7.pdf

[6] Carl Levin. United States Senator. Agriculture on the Issues. (n.d.). Retrieved September 26, 2010, from http://www.levin.senate.gov/issues/index.cfm?MainIssue=Agriculture

[6] National Agricultural Statistics Service. USDA Michigan Field Office. Retrieved September 26, 2010, from http://www.michiganwines.com/page.php?menu_id=19

[7] Michigan Brewers Guild. (n.d.). Retrieved September 26, 2010, from http://michiganbrewersguild.businesscatalyst.com

Cooking is ancient art which is continually evolving. Accordingly, recipes have been designed to be flexible in nature and include ingredients which are interchangeable. Some ideas for ingredient substitution are reviewed below.

Sweeteners can be interchanged but keep in mind it might change the flavor profile of a dish. When adding sweetness experiment with honey, maple syrup, agave or pure cane sugar instead of refined table sugar. Natural sweeteners not only add flavor but also increases the nutritional value of your food.

Acids such as vinegars and certain fruit juices can be interchanged as well. Substitutions for vinegars can include balsamic, red wine, apple cider, raspberry, cherry and blueberry, or to enhance citrus flavor add fruit juices such as lemon, lime, and orange. A great example of how to utilize different acids is shown in the recipe for "Flexible Salsa" on page 37.

Grains including barley, rice, quinoa, farro and wheat berries can all be interchanged, but keep in mind that these grains all have very different textures and flavors. Quinoa, rice and risotto also are excellent gluten-free alternatives.

Dressings and **marinades** are also interchangeable. The small plates section includes many salads in which the dressings can be interchanged, or even used as marinades. The proteins section has been created with interchangeable marinades that compliment many different types of meat, poultry and fish.

Fats can also be interchanged. If your trying to reduce your consumption of animal products, use plant based oils such as olive, coconut or peanut oils instead of butter. Fat substitutions are not recommended for baking unless your an advanced baker.

Salting your food can be eliminated by garnishing your meal with salty toppings including salty cheese, capers, olives and anchovies or liquids such as soy sauce and Braggs Amino Acids. If you really need to salt your food then sprinkle cooking salt or finishing salt over your meal. This will add both flavor and texture. Using any of these methods increases the nutritional value of your food over traditional iodized table salt.

Creating something delicious for yourself, your guests or your family can be a sublime experience. Just try what you believe might be delicious, and it will always be a beautiful experiment.

SMALL PLATES

CHAPTER
No. 4

Beet & Arugula Salad
──◦ serves 6 ◦──

Beets and arugula peak during the late spring and fall. This salad features the contrasting flavors and textures of naturally sweet beets, spicy arugula, and creamy goat cheese. The citrus dressing is delicious on any salad. Raw or roasted beets can be used. It's your preference.

INGREDIENTS

citrus dressing
¼ cup extra-virgin olive oil
4 tablespoons orange juice, freshly squeezed
1 garlic clove, finely chopped
Salt and pepper

salad
1 tablespoon extra-virgin olive oil
6-8 red or yellow beets, scrubbed and trimmed ½ inch from top
1 bunch arugula

optional garnishes
½ cup feta cheese (goat or sheep), coarsely crumbled
½ onion, thinly sliced
4 radishes, thinly sliced

PREPARATION

1. Preheat oven to 425°F.

2. To make the dressing, use a glass jar with a removable lid and add all dressing ingredients. Season with salt and freshly ground pepper and shake well.

3. *Raw preparation:* To prepare the raw beets, shred using a hand grater or a vegetable slicer.

4. *Roasted preparation:* In an 11 x 17-inch baking pan, toss beets with 1 tablespoon of olive oil. Roast beets until tender, about 1 hour. Allow beets to cool. Peel and cut into bite-sized wedges, or thinly slice.

5. Place arugula in a large bowl and coat with dressing. Divide among plates and arrange the beets on the greens.

6. Season with salt and pepper to taste.

7. Add desired garnishes.

Gorgonzola & Pears with Mixed Greens
—◌ serves 6 ◌—

INGREDIENTS

lemon dressing
1 lemon juiced, about 3 tablespoons
1 tablespoon Dijon mustard
1 medium shallot, finely chopped
1 teaspoon fresh thyme, finely chopped
1 garlic clove, finely chopped
⅓ cup extra-virgin olive oil
Salt and pepper

salad
1 large bunch watercress, arugula, baby spinach, or mixed greens
½ sweet onion, thinly sliced
2 large ripe pears, halved, cored, thinly sliced lengthwise (coat with lemon juice to prevent browning)
1 cup Gorgonzola cheese, crumbled
1 cup walnuts, coarsely chopped
½ cup dried fruit (blueberries, cherries, cranberries)
¼ cup sunflower or pumpkin seeds

PREPARATION

1. To make the dressing, use a glass jar with a removable lid and add all dressing ingredients. Season with salt and freshly ground pepper and shake well.

2. In a large bowl, toss the greens with dressing.

3. Divide greens among 6 salad bowls or plates. Garnish with a few rings of sweet onion. Top each salad with several pear slices. Sprinkle with cheese, walnuts, dried fruit and seeds. Drizzle with more dressing, if necessary.

Tangy Yogurt Cheese
—◌ serves 6 ◌—

INGREDIENTS
1 quart Greek-style or Lebanese yogurt (do not use fat-free)
Salt to taste
6 pitas, cut into wedges, or 1 package mini pitas
½ cup Greek olive mix

PREPARATION

1. Line a large sieve with a layer of cheesecloth, and place it over a large bowl.

2. Mix yogurt and salt together. Pour the mixture into the lined sieve and strain in the refrigerator for 12-24 hours. The longer the yogurt is strained, the thicker it will become.

3. Serve with warm pitas and Greek olive mix.

Roasted Red Pepper Dip
serves 6

INGREDIENTS
½ cup walnuts, lightly toasted
5 fresh medium red peppers, roasted or 1 16-ounce jar roasted red peppers
1 tablespoon extra-virgin olive oil
½ cup bread crumbs
2 garlic cloves, finely chopped
1 teaspoon ground cumin
½ teaspoon red pepper flakes or ¼ teaspoon cayenne pepper
2 teaspoons pomegranate molasses or balsamic vinegar
1 tablespoon extra-virgin olive oil
1 tablespoon lemon juice
1 head romaine, leaves (removed and cleaned), and/or 6 pita bread wedges

PREPARATION
1. Preheat the oven to 350°F.

2. Toast walnuts in the oven for 10 minutes. Cool and finely chop.

3. To roast the peppers, coat the peppers with olive oil and place them on a sheet pan in the oven for 30 minutes, or until tender. For easy removal of the skins, place the warm peppers in a large covered bowl for 15 minutes. A large salad bowl using a plate as a cover works well. Remove the skins, stem, and seeds.

4. In a food processor, blend the walnuts, roasted peppers, bread crumbs, garlic, cumin, red pepper flakes, pomegranate molasses, olive oil, and lemon until smooth.

5. Serve with romaine lettuce leaves or pita bread wedges, or both.

Shredded Root Salad
serves 6

INGREDIENTS
1½ pounds sweet carrots, or fennel
⅓ cup lemon juice, freshly squeezed
½ cup extra-virgin olive oil
¼ cup parsley, finely chopped
Salt and pepper

PREPARATION
1. Using carrots, use a hand grater to shred or julienne, resulting in thin strips like cole slaw. Using fennel, trim off the top of the bulb and shave fennel lengthwise using a vegetable slicer, mandolin or a very sharp knife. Place vegetables in medium bowl.

2. Add the lemon juice, olive oil, and parsley. Toss well and season with salt and pepper to taste. Set aside to allow flavors to blend.

Note: Shredded root salad is also delicious as a topping on salads or sandwiches.

Flexible Salsa
⚬ 2 cups ⚬

Flexible salsa is easy to make with a variety of interchangeable ingredients. The formula includes a main fruit (mango, peach, cherry, or tomato), an acid (lemon, lime, or vinegar), fresh green herbs (mint, basil, or cilantro) and a spice (habañero, red pepper flakes, or jalapeño). The ingredients in these recipes can be interchanged, depending on your mood. Canned, fire-roasted tomatoes can be substituted when fresh tomatoes are not available. Salsas are also delicious toppings for grilled fish or chicken.

INGREDIENTS

1 bag blue corn chips

mango or peach salsa

2 mangos or 4 peaches, pitted, peeled, and diced (about 2 cups)
1 small red bell pepper, diced
1 lime, juiced
3 tablespoons basil, finely chopped
1 habañero (optional, for extreme heat)

cherry salsa

2 cups cherries, cleaned and pitted
3 tablespoons red onion, finely chopped
1 lemon, juiced
3 tablespoons mint, chopped
2 garlic cloves, finely chopped
½ teaspoon red pepper flakes

tomato salsa

5 large tomatoes, diced, or a 28-ounce can of diced, fire-roasted tomatoes
3 garlic cloves, finely chopped
2 tablespoons apple cider vinegar
1 teaspoon cumin
1 jalapeño, finely chopped
¼ cup cilantro, finely chopped
¼ cup green onions, sliced

optional garnishes

1 avocado, sliced or diced
12 shrimp, precooked
Hot sauce
4 green onions, sliced

PREPARATION

1. Chop ingredients according to desired recipe. If you're using habañeros or jalapeños, use rubber gloves and wash hands well afterward.

2. Combine all ingredients in a bowl.

3. Garnish as desired.

4. Serve with blue corn chips.

Green Bean Salad
serves 6

INGREDIENTS

spicy vinaigrette dressing
  2 garlic cloves, finely chopped
  3 tablespoons extra-virgin olive oil
  1 lime, juiced, or 2 tablespoons of red wine vinegar
  ½ cup cilantro or Italian parsley, chopped
  ½ teaspoon red pepper flakes
  Salt and pepper

salad
  2 pounds green beans, trimmed
  2 green onions, finely chopped (about 2 tablespoons)

PREPARATION
1. To make the dressing, use a glass jar with a removable lid and add all dressing ingredients. Season with salt and freshly ground pepper and shake well.

2. Boil 1-inch water in a medium stockpot. Using a steamer insert, cook beans until tender but still crisp, about 4 minutes. Transfer beans to a colander and rinse under cold water to stop the cooking process. Drain beans well.

3. In a large bowl, combine beans, green onions, and dressing; then toss well. Serve cold.

Cucumber & Tomato Salad
serves 6

INGREDIENTS

red wine vinegar dressing
  ¼ cup extra-virgin olive oil
  3 tablespoons red wine vinegar
  2 garlic cloves, finely chopped
  ¼ cup basil or oregano, finely chopped
  Salt and pepper

salad
  3 tomatoes, cut into wedges
  2 cucumbers, peeled and roughly chopped
  1 yellow or red pepper, roughly chopped
  4 green onions, thinly sliced
  ½ cup feta cheese (goat or sheep), coarsely crumbled

PREPARATION
1. To make the dressing, use a glass jar with a removable lid and add all dressing ingredients. Season with salt and freshly ground pepper and shake well.

2. In a large bowl, combine tomatoes, cucumbers, peppers, and green onions. Add the dressing and toss well. Sprinkle with feta.

Greens with Michigan Smoked Fish
serves 6

INGREDIENTS

lemon dill dressing
4 tablespoons extra-virgin olive oil
3 tablespoons lemon juice
¼ cup fresh dill, chopped
Salt and pepper

salad
6 cups watercress or arugula, trimmed
½ cup red onion, thinly sliced
2 red apples, cored and thinly sliced (coat with lemon juice to prevent browning)
8 ounces smoked trout, salmon, or whitefish, remove skin and coarsely flake
¼ cup blueberries

PREPARATION
1. To make the dressing, use a glass jar with a removable lid and add all dressing ingredients. Season with salt and freshly ground pepper and shake well.

2. In large bowl, add watercress or arugula and half of the dressing; toss to coat.

3. Mound greens in center of each plate or bowl. Top salad with onion slices, apple slices, fish and blueberries. Spoon additional dressing over the salad, if necessary.

Horseradish Smashed Potatoes
serves 6

INGREDIENTS
2 pounds russet potatoes, washed
½ cup heavy cream
½ stick butter (4 tablespoons)
4 tablespoons prepared horseradish, or 3 tablespoons wasabi paste
4 green onions, sliced
Salt and pepper

PREPARATION
1. Preheat oven to 400°F.

2. On a sheet pan, bake potatoes for about 1 hour or until soft.

3. In a medium stockpot, add potatoes, cream, butter, and horseradish or wasabi. Using potato masher, smash until creamy. For spicier flavor, add more horseradish or wasabi.

4. Top with green onions. Season to taste with salt and freshly ground pepper.

Note: You can remove potato skins if desired, but doing so removes important nutrients.

Prosciutto-Wrapped Asparagus
~ serves 6 ~

Imagine smoky prosciutto wrapping crispy asparagus, drizzled with balsamic vinaigrette and topped with Gorgonzola. This is a rich appetizer that is simple to create.

INGREDIENTS

1 pound asparagus, trimmed
16 prosciutto slices, thinly sliced
¼ cup extra-virgin olive oil
3 tablespoons balsamic vinegar
½ cup Gorgonzola cheese or blue cheese, crumbled

PREPARATION

1. Boil 1-inch water in a medium stockpot. Using a steamer insert, steam asparagus for 6-8 minutes. Immediately run cold water over asparagus to stop the cooking process. Asparagus should be crisp. Cool completely.

2. Wrap 3-5 asparagus pieces with 1-2 prosciutto pieces, leaving the tips exposed.

3. Arrange on a platter; then drizzle with olive oil and balsamic vinegar.

4. Top with cheese. Serve at room temperature.

Roasted Cauliflower with Tahini Dressing
~ serves 6 ~

INGREDIENTS

Tahini dressing
3 garlic cloves, finely chopped
1 inch ginger root, remove skin and slice thinly
¼ cup tahini paste
¼ cup water
3 tablespoons lemon juice
2 tablespoons soy sauce
1 teaspoon honey

roasted cauliflower
1 tablespoon extra-virgin olive oil
1 large cauliflower head, broken into bite-size pieces
¼ cup cilantro or parsley, finely chopped
Salt and pepper

PREPARATION

1. To make the dressing, use a glass jar with a removable lid and add all dressing ingredients. Season with salt and freshly ground pepper and shake well. For better flavor, make a day ahead. Store in the refrigerator. Remove ginger slices before using.

2. Preheat oven to 400°F. On a baking sheet, coat cauliflower with olive oil and roast until tender and crispy, about 35 minutes. Turn once or twice during cooking.

3. Remove cauliflower from oven. Immediately transfer to a serving bowl. Pour the Tahini sauce over the cauliflower, and toss to combine. Sprinkle with cilantro or parsley. Season with salt and freshly ground pepper.

Kale Salad
serves 6

This recipe is best made a day before serving to allow the kale to soften. Kale is a nutrient-dense vegetable, high in beta carotene, vitamin K, vitamin C, lutein, and calcium. This recipe can also be made with other dark greens such as Asian greens, spinach, or cooking greens. Visit page 22 for a detailed list.

INGREDIENTS

soy citrus dressing
¼ cup lemon juice, freshly squeezed
¼ cup low-sodium soy sauce
¼ cup olive or sesame oil
1 teaspoon red pepper flakes

salad
1 bunch kale*, ribs removed
1 cup sun gold or cherry tomatoes, cut into halves
¼ cup green onions, sliced into coins
¼ cup sunflower or pumpkin seeds

PREPARATION

1. To make the dressing, use a glass jar with a removable lid and add all dressing ingredients. Shake well.

2. Remove the ribs from the kale and chop into bite-size pieces. Place in a large bowl.

3. Add the tomatoes and green onions, and toss with dressing. Sprinkle with sunflower or pumpkin seeds.

   *Lacinato kale is softer than the other varieties and will need less time to marinate.

SOUPS

CHAPTER
No. 5

Tom Yummy Soup
—☙ serves 8 ☙—

Sweet, salty, sour, and spicy! The contrasting flavors of this light, fragrant soup will leave your taste buds tingling. Other vegetables can be added. Serve with sticky rice.

INGREDIENTS

1 lemongrass stalk*
8 cups chicken or vegetable stock
2 large garlic cloves, finely chopped
2 tablespoons fish sauce*
4 kaffir lime leaves*, fresh or frozen
2 inches galangal* or ginger, peeled and thinly sliced
2 tablespoons lime juice
1 tablespoon sugar
1 pint cherry tomatoes, halved
¾ cup snow peas
¾ cup mushrooms, thinly sliced
1 jalapeño, thinly sliced
½ pound chicken, shrimp or tofu, cut into 1 inch pieces
⅓ cup cilantro, chopped
4 green onions, thinly sliced

PREPARATION

1. To prepare the lemongrass, remove the tough outer layer and slice 1-2 inches off the root end. Using the firm part of the stalk, slice into 1/2-inch pieces.

2. In a large stockpot, add the stock, lemongrass, garlic, fish sauce, lime leaves, galangal, lime juice, and sugar. Simmer uncovered for 45 minutes. For a stronger flavor, refrigerate overnight.

3. Strain the stock using a fine-mesh sieve, then discard the solids.

4. Add cherry tomatoes, snow peas, mushrooms, and jalapeño to the hot stock and simmer for three minutes. Vegetables should remain crisp.

5. Add the cooked shrimp or chicken. For a vegetarian version, omit the fish sauce and add tofu. Simmer for five minutes.

6. Sprinkle with cilantro and green onions.

* These items are available at Asian markets. Fish sauce is often labeled as nam pla or nuoc mam.

Egg Lemon Soup
serves 8

Greek inspired, this is the ultimate comfort soup, perfect for a winter day. The thick and tangy soup is simple to make using but a few ingredients. One important tip: after adding the eggs, constantly stir the soup to prevent the eggs from separating. For a gluten-free alternative, substitute the orzo with white rice.

INGREDIENTS

3 cups water
1 cup orzo or white rice
4 large eggs
3 lemons, freshly squeezed
8 cups chicken or vegetable stock
Salt and pepper

PREPARATION

1. In a medium stockpot, bring three cups of water to a boil, add the orzo, and cook on medium heat until it's tender, about 20 minutes.

2. In a medium bowl, beat the eggs and lemon juice with a whisk until they are light and frothy.

3. Once the orzo is cooked, drain using a fine-mesh strainer. Place the orzo in a medium bowl and set aside. It will be added back into the soup toward the end of cooking.

4. Using a large stockpot, add the stock and bring to a boil over medium-high heat. Then reduce the heat to medium-low.

5. Gradually ladle 2 cups of the hot stock into the egg and lemon mixture, constantly stirring with a whisk until it's well mixed. This ensures that the egg-lemon mixture will not curdle.

6. Slowly add the diluted egg-lemon mixture to the stockpot, constantly stirring with a whisk for about 15-20 minutes. Bring almost to the boiling point. The soup should thicken to the consistency of a thin custard.

7. Once the soup has thickened, add the orzo back into the soup.

8. Remove the soup from the heat, cover the stockpot and allow to rest for 20 minutes. This allows the soup to thicken further.

9. Add salt and freshly ground pepper to taste.

Black Bean Soup
serves 8

Creamy black bean soup is comforting on a cool fall or winter day. For a vegetarian option, use vegetable stock. For a complete meal, serve with a grain such as quinoa, rice, or barley.

INGREDIENTS
1 pound dry black beans, cooked, or 2 15-ounce cans black beans
2 tablespoons extra-virgin olive oil
1 cup onion, chopped
½ cup carrots, chopped
4 garlic cloves, chopped
1 tablespoon ground cumin
1 teaspoon chili powder
1 jalapeño, sliced or diced
2 cups tomatoes, chopped or 1 15-ounce can diced tomatoes with juice
2 cups chicken or vegetable stock
1 teaspoon Worcestershire sauce
¼ cup tomato paste
Salt and pepper

optional garnishes
¼ cup fresh cilantro, chopped
¼ cup green onions, chopped
¼ cup red peppers, chopped
¼ cup feta cheese, crumbled
1 avocado, peeled and sliced

PREPARATION
1. If using dry beans, then follow the instruction on the package.

2. Over medium-high heat, using a large stockpot, heat the olive oil; then add the onion, carrot, and garlic. Sauté until vegetables begin to soften, about 6 minutes. Stir in the cumin, chili powder, and one half of the jalapeño.

3. Add cooked beans, tomatoes with juice, stock, Worcestershire sauce, and tomato paste; bring soup to boil. Reduce heat to medium, cover, and cook until carrots are tender, about 15 minutes.

4. For a smooth soup, use an immersion blender* to purée. Strain soup through a sieve to remove the skins. Return purée to stockpot. Simmer soup until slightly thickened, about 15 minutes. Skip this step if you like a chunkier soup.

5. Add remaining jalapeño, if desired. Season with salt and freshly ground pepper to taste.

6. Garnish with one or all of the optional garnishes.

* An immersion blender is a hand blender. A regular blender or food processor can also be used.

Gazpacho
serves 8

Gazpacho is a cold Spanish soup, perfect for a hot summer day. Gazpacho is widely consumed throughout Spain, Portugal, and Latin American countries. It descends from an ancient Andalusian soup based on a combination of stale bread, garlic, extra-virgin olive oil, salt, and vinegar. In the United States, most gazpacho recipes include tomato, cucumber, bell pepper, onion, garlic, and celery. Other recipes also include olive oil, bread, vinegar or lemon juice, fresh herbs, sugar, canned tomato juice, or hot sauce. Gazpacho can be puréed until smooth or served chunky style.

INGREDIENTS

3 cups fresh tomatoes, diced
½ cup yellow pepper, diced
1 cup cucumber, diced
½ cup sweet onion, diced
3 cloves garlic, finely chopped
¼ cup cilantro, finely chopped
1 lemon or lime, juiced
¼ cup red wine vinegar
⅓ cup extra-virgin olive oil
2 tablespoons Worcestershire sauce
1 32–ounce jar spicy tomato juice
½ cup plain bread crumbs
Salt and pepper

optional garnishes
¼ cup cilantro, chopped
1 avocado, sliced
12 shrimp, whole, cooked, and peeled

PREPARATION

1. In a large bowl, combine the tomatoes, pepper, cucumber, onion, garlic, cilantro, lemon or lime juice, red wine vinegar, olive oil, and Worcestershire sauce.

2. Pour the tomato juice into the vegetable mixture. Add bread crumbs and stir until they dissolve into the liquid.

3. If you prefer a smooth soup, use an immersion blender* to purée.

4. Season with salt and freshly ground pepper. Garnish if desired.

Note: An immersion blender is a hand blender. A regular blender or food processor can also be used.

Lentil & Chard Soup
∼ serves 8 ∼

This reminds me of my grandmother's recipe, a light and flavorful soup packed full of dark leafy greens and lentils.

INGREDIENTS

1½ cups dried lentils, french green*
6-8 cups chicken stock
3 tablespoons extra-virgin olive oil
1 large onion, finely chopped
4 garlic cloves, finely chopped
2 large carrots, sliced into ½ inch rounds
Pinch of crushed red pepper
½ cup cilantro, coarsely chopped
1 bunch cooking greens, swiss chard, beet greens, or kale, ribs removed and coarsely chopped
⅓ cup lemon juice
½ cup Parmigiano-Reggiano cheese
Salt and pepper

PREPARATION

1. In a medium saucepan, combine the lentils with stock and bring to a boil. Cover partially and cook over moderately low heat until the lentils are barely tender, about 20-25 minutes.

2. Meanwhile, heat the olive oil in a large sauté pan over medium heat. Add the onion, garlic, carrot, and crushed red pepper, stirring occasionally until the onion is lightly browned, 7 to 8 minutes. Add half of the cilantro, and cook for 1 minute.

3. Add the mixture to stock, cover partially, and simmer until thickened, Add the cooking greens, stirring occasionally until wilted. Stir in the lemon juice. Cook for an additional 10 minutes.

4. Ladle the soup into bowls. Garnish with remaining cilantro and Parmigiano-Reggiano.

5. Season to taste with salt and freshly ground pepper.

French green lentils are the firmest lentil, making it perfect for Lentil and Chard soup. Brown lentils shown in the photo can be used also. Pink lentils will result in a creamy, textured soup; therefore, I do not recommend them.

Creamy Squash Soup
serves 8

This bright, creamy soup warms your soul on a gloomy fall or winter day.
Squash soup is easy to make and has an exquisite flavor.

INGREDIENTS
6 cups butternut squash (2 small squash)
⅓ cup extra-virgin olive oil
1 large onion, finely chopped
4 garlic cloves, chopped
1 green apple, cored and diced
6 cups chicken or vegetable stock
1¼ teaspoons fresh thyme, finely chopped
1¼ teaspoons fresh sage, finely chopped
½ teaspoon nutmeg
½ cup heavy cream or unsweetened coconut milk
Salt and pepper

optional garnishes
4 green onions, thinly sliced
½ cup feta cheese (goat or sheep), coarsely crumbled

PREPARATION
1. Preheat oven to 400°F. Cut squash in half lengthwise and place face down on a sheet pan. Place pan in oven and add 1/2-inch water to the bottom of pan. This allows the squash to steam and not dry out. Bake for about 45 minutes, or until tender.

2. Allow squash to cool. Remove seeds with a spoon and discard. Then remove flesh from the skin with a spoon and set aside.

3. In a large stockpot, over medium heat, add the olive oil, onion, garlic, and apple. Sauté until tender, about 10 minutes. Add the squash, stock, herbs, and nutmeg. Bring to a boil, then reduce heat, cover, and simmer until squash is very tender, about 30 minutes.

4. To purée, use an immersion blender*.

5. Stir in cream or coconut milk; bring to simmer. Garnish if desired.

6. Season with salt and freshly ground pepper.

* An immersion blender is a hand blender. A regular blender or food processor can also be used.

Michigan Three Bean Veggie Chili
～ serves 8 ～

Michigan is the second largest producer of all dry beans in the United States, including black, cranberry, great northern, navy, kidney, pinto, and yellow eye. Any combination of these beans are delicious in this chili recipe. For a complete meal, serve with a grain such as farro, rice, or wheat berries.

INGREDIENTS

beans

3 cups dried beans, assorted varieties
9 cups water
1 teaspoon salt
1 teaspoon onion powder
1 teaspoon garlic powder
1 teaspoon sweet paprika
1 teaspoon Italian seasoning
1 teaspoon chili powder
2 bay leaves
1 teaspoon chipotle pepper flakes
1 tablespoon cumin

chili

1 small acorn squash
2 tablespoons extra-virgin olive oil
1 red onion, diced
4 garlic cloves, minced
2 carrots, sliced into ½ inch rounds
1 small green pepper, diced
4-8 cups vegetable stock, add more for thinner chili
1 32-ounce can fire-roasted tomatoes
3 tablespoons tomato paste
2 tablespoons apple cider vinegar
1 teaspoon chipotle pepper flakes
3 tablespoons chili powder
1 tablespoon cumin
1 teaspoon coriander
¼ teaspoon cinnamon
½ teaspoon salt
1 bunch kale (ribs removed), finely chopped
½ cup cilantro, finely chopped

garnishes

¼ cup fresh cilantro, chopped
¼ cup feta cheese, crumbled
1 avocado, peeled and sliced
3 greens onions, sliced

PREPARATION

1. Soak the beans overnight. Rinse well before using.

2. Cook the beans in a large stockpot over high heat. Add the water, beans, and spices and bring to a boil. Then reduce to a simmer for 2 hours, until beans become tender. Add more water if necessary. When finished cooking, drain and rinse beans.

3. To roast the squash, preheat the oven to 400°F. Cut the squash in half and place face down on a sheet pan. Place the squash in the oven and add 1/2-inch water to the bottom of pan. This allows the squash to steam and not dry out. Bake for about 45 minutes, until tender. Allow squash to cool. Remove seeds with a spoon and discard. Remove the flesh, place in a large bowl and mash. Then set aside.

4. In a large stockpot using medium-high heat, add the olive oil, onion, garlic, carrots, and green pepper. Sauté until vegetables begin to soften, about 10 minutes.

5. Add the vegetable stock, beans, tomatoes with juice, tomato paste, squash, and vinegar.

6. Stir in the chipotle, chili powder, cumin, coriander, cinnamon, and salt.

7. Reduce heat to low, and cook for 1 hour.

8. Add kale and cilantro and continue cooking for an additional 15 minutes.

9. Garnish if desired.

Creamy Tomato Soup
serves 8

Tomato soup is delicious paired with the Grilled Cheese Sandwich, the recipe is on page 83.

INGREDIENTS

10 medium tomatoes, roasted, or 2 28-ounce cans of fire-roasted tomatoes, diced
2 tablespoons extra-virgin olive oil
2 celery sticks, sliced into ½ inch pieces
2 large carrots, sliced into ½ inch rounds
1 onion, diced
2 garlic cloves, finely chopped
3 tablespoons tomato paste
1 tablespoon basil, finely chopped
3 cups chicken or vegetable stock
4-6 ounces chèvre goat cheese
Salt and pepper

PREPARATION

1. To roast the tomatoes, preheat the oven to 375°F. Cut the tomatoes in half, core, and slice into chunks. Place the mixture onto a sheet pan and drizzle with 1 tablespoon olive oil. Use clean hands to combine. Place the mixture in the hot oven for 30 minutes, until softened.

2. Meanwhile, in a large stockpot over medium-low heat, heat the olive oil, and then add the celery, carrot, onion, and garlic. Cook until softened and translucent, approximately 7-10 minutes.

3. Add the oven-roasted or fire-roasted tomatoes with juices, tomato paste, basil, and stock to the stockpot.

4. Simmer until vegetables are very tender, about 15 to 20 minutes.

5. Add the goat cheese and stir until melted. For an ultra smooth soup, purée using an immersion blender* and then pour through a strainer.

6. Season with salt and freshly ground pepper.

An immersion blender is a hand blender. A regular blender or food processor can also be used.

Roasted Pepper Soup
serves 8

Roasted pepper soup is delicious served cold or hot. Use any color bell pepper...green, red, orange, purple or yellow. Be sure to make the soup a day ahead to allow the flavors to blend.

INGREDIENTS
5 pounds bell peppers, whole
2 jalapeños, whole
2 large sweet onions, chopped
6 garlic cloves, finely chopped
2 tablespoon extra-virgin olive oil
3 cups vegetable stock
1 cup apple juice or cider
⅛ teaspoon red pepper flakes
Salt and pepper

optional garnishes
¼ cup fresh basil, chopped
½ cup chèvre goat cheese
⅛ teaspoon red pepper flakes

PREPARATION
1. Preheat oven to 350°F. On a sheet pan, place the bell peppers, jalapeños, onions and garlic. Add olive oil and turn vegetable mixture until it's evenly coated in oil, using clean hands. Roast the vegetables for 30 minutes, or until tender.

2. For easy removal of the skins, place the warm peppers in a large covered bowl for 15 minutes. (A large salad bowl using a plate as a cover works well.) Remove peppers from bowl and remove the skins, stem, and seeds.

3. In a stockpot over medium heat, add the roasted vegetables, apple juice and red pepper flakes to the vegetable stock. Cook for 15 minutes.

4. Use an immersion blender* to purée the soup. If you desire an extremely smooth soup, then pour puréed soup through a strainer.

5. Season with salt and freshly ground pepper.

6. Garnish if desired.

An immersion blender is a hand blender. A regular blender or food processor can also be used.

Potato Leek Soup
serves 8

A steaming bowl of potato soup, gently suggestive of leeks, is warming after a cold day playing in the snow. For the vegetarian version, use vegetable stock and skip the bacon.

INGREDIENTS

3 pounds potatoes, washed
2 pounds medium leeks
¾ pound cooked bacon, crumbled
¼ cup extra virgin olive-oil or bacon fat
1 medium celeriac root, peeled and diced
1 medium onion, diced
2 large carrots, sliced into ½ inch rounds
2 celery stalks, sliced into ½ inch pieces
4 garlic cloves, minced
8 cups chicken or vegetable stock
4 bay leaves
1 teaspoon thyme
1 teaspoon white ground pepper
½ cup dry white wine (optional)
Salt and pepper

optional garnishes

1 cup sour cream
4 green onions, thinly sliced
¼ pound cooked bacon, finely chopped

PREPARATION

1. Preheat oven to 400°F. Bake potatoes for 1 hour, until tender. Allow to cool, then mash the potatoes using a potato masher or ricer.

2. Meanwhile, using a sharp knife, halve the white part of the leeks lengthwise, and rinse well under cold running water to remove any sand. Slice thinly crosswise and set aside. Discard green portions.

3. Cook the bacon according to the directions on the packaging. If desired, reserve the fat to sauté the vegetables.

4. In same pan, heat 1-3 tablespoons of bacon fat or olive oil over medium heat. Add the leeks, celeriac root, onion, carrot, celery, and garlic, stirring occasionally until softened. Transfer to a large stockpot.

5. Add the stock, mashed potatoes, bay leaves, thyme, white pepper, and wine. Bring to a boil. Then reduce heat and simmer, covered, until vegetables are tender, about 45 minutes.

6. Blend soup with a immersion blender until smooth, about 1-3 minutes. Add 3/4 cup cooked bacon, stir, and then cover pan. Return heat to a simmer for 45 minutes.

7. Garnish if desired.

8. Season with salt and freshly ground pepper.

PASTA & PIZZA

CHAPTER
No. 6

Homemade Pasta
serves 6

Homemade pasta has a richer flavor and silkier texture than dried store-bought pasta, it's delicious to eat with just butter and cheese. This recipe is great for any type of pasta – tagliolini (1/8 inch wide), tagliatelle (1/4 inch wide), fettuccine (1/2 inch wide), pappardelle (3/4 inch wide), or lasagna noodles. Pasta can be created by mixing a variety of flours creating different flavors and textures. If you don't own a pasta machine, don't worry! A rolling pin, a knife and some muscle will do. This is a great upper body workout!

basic pasta

3 cups all-purpose flour or semolina
½ teaspoon salt
4 large eggs, beaten
water

multi-flour pasta

1½ cups all-purpose flour
¾ cup semolina
¾ cup chestnut flour
½ teaspoon salt
4 large eggs, beaten
water

PREPARATION

Using a large bowl, sift the flour and salt into a mound and make a well in the center. Add the eggs to the well. Using your hands gradually incorporate the flour. Once the dough is incorporated, start kneading it with your hands. If the dough is dry, then add one tablespoon of water and continue working the dough. Continue this process until the dough is easily formed into a smooth ball, about 5 minutes. Wrap in plastic and allow it to rest at room temperature for one hour. Next, prepare a flat clean work surface.

ROLLING DOUGH INTO SHEETS

Step 1 - Shape dough into a long roll about 12 inches long, like French bread. Divide dough into 4 equal pieces. Cover with plastic wrap.

Step 2 - Flatten one piece of dough into a rectangle with a rolling pin. Run the dough through the pasta machine on the highest setting twice. If don't have a pasta machine, flour your flat work surface and use a rolling pin roll out the dough twice.

Step 3 - Continue making the dough thinner. Adjust the pasta machine to a smaller setting after each pass. To keep pasta from sticking, dust with flour as needed. To roll out by hand, continue working the dough with a rolling pin until you reach the desired thickness, about 1/16-inch. Pasta sheets should measure about 20 inches long. Place sheets on a lightly floured work surface and cover with plastic wrap or towels. Repeat with remaining pasta pieces.

CUTTING DOUGH INTO STRANDS

Uncover pasta sheets. Fit machine with appropriate pasta cutter or use a sharp well-oiled knife. Run pasta sheets through machine or hand cut to desired thickness, dusting pasta with flour to keep it from sticking. Cut strands crosswise into desired lengths. Using floured hands, toss strands to separate; spread out on towels or wire drying racks.

TO COOK

Cook fresh pasta in a stockpot of boiling water 3-5 minutes, until tender. Stir occasionally. Drain and serve.

Step 1

Step 2

Step 3

Hearty Lasagna
serves 8

Ground buffalo or lamb gives this dish a rich, flavorful twist. For a lower-fat option, use buffalo with low-fat ricotta. Lasagna can be prepared up to 1 day ahead and then cooked the following day. This sauce is also delicious for homemade pasta or polenta.

INGREDIENTS

sauce
¼ cup extra-virgin olive oil
1 pound ground lamb, buffalo, or beef (or a mixture)
1 cup onion, diced
¾ cup carrots, cut into ½ inch rounds
4 garlic cloves, minced
1 32-ounce can tomatoes diced with basil
1 tablespoon balsamic vinegar
1 teaspoon oregano
½ teaspoon red pepper flakes
¼ cup fresh basil, chopped
10 basil stems

pasta
15-20 lasagna noodles, (see pasta recipe on page 66) or one package of store-bought

filling
4 cups ricotta cheese (see recipe on page 121)
1 10-ounce package frozen chopped spinach, drained
2 large eggs
½ teaspoon nutmeg
2 cups mozzarella, sliced thinly
1 cup goat or feta cheese, crumbled
½ cup Parmigiano-Reggiano

PREPARATION

1. To make the sauce, over medium heat add 2 tablespoons oil to a large saucepan. Add the meat and sauté until cooked, breaking up the meat with the back of a spoon, about 5 minutes. Drain the oil and set meat aside.

2. In the same pan, heat the remainder of the oil and add onion, carrots, and garlic; sauté until softened, about 10 minutes. Add the cooked meat, tomatoes, vinegar, oregano, red pepper flakes, basil, and basil stems. Simmer for about 60 minutes, stirring occasionally until flavors blend. Allow sauce to cool, then remove basil stems.

3. Boil water and cook pasta. Cook fresh homemade pasta 3-5 minutes. If using store-bought pasta, follow the directions on the package. Drain pasta well.

4. For the filling, combine ricotta, spinach, eggs, and nutmeg in a medium bowl.

5. To bake lasagna, preheat oven to 375°F.

6. Spread 1/2 cup sauce over bottom of 9 x 13-inch glass baking dish. Place noodles over sauce, overlapping to fit. Trim noodles if needed. Spread ricotta-spinach filling evenly over noodles; then add another layer of noodles. Spread sauce over noodles; add mozzarella and goat cheese. Repeat layering until even with top of the pan. Add a final layer of sauce and sprinkle Parmigiano-Reggiano. You should have three or four layers of lasagna noodles.

7. Cover dish with aluminum foil, and bake lasagna for 40 minutes. Remove foil from lasagna and continue baking until hot and bubbly, about 40 more minutes. Allow lasagna to stand 15 minutes before serving.

Light Summer Sauce
serves 6

This light but flavorful summer and fall dish uses vine-ripened tomatoes, other seasonal produce, and herbs. Light Summer Sauce is the perfect companion to homemade pasta (see recipe on page 66). To save time, store-bought pasta can also be used.

INGREDIENTS

3 tablespoons extra-virgin olive oil
2 garlic cloves, finely chopped
½ cup sweet onion, chopped
1 yellow pepper, chopped
¼ cup white wine or vermouth
½ cup mushrooms, sliced
½ teaspoon red pepper flakes
1 pint red cherry tomatoes, sliced in half
1 pint yellow cherry tomatoes, sliced in half
1 full pasta recipe, see page 66, or 1 package store-bought
½ cup basil, chopped
½ cup Parmigiano-Reggiano cheese
Salt and pepper

PREPARATION

1. In medium stockpot, boil water and then add pasta, cooking until just tender but still firm to bite, about 3-5 minutes. Cook store-bought pasta according to instructions on the package. Drain pasta well.

2. Meanwhile, heat oil in a heavy large skillet over medium-high heat. Add garlic, onion, and yellow pepper, and sauté about 2 minutes.

3. Add wine, mushrooms, and red pepper flakes then sauté until slightly softened, about 2 minutes. Add tomatoes and sauté about 1 minute, until warm.

4. Add desired amount of sauce to the pasta, and add fresh basil. Serve with Parmigiano-Reggiano.

5. Season with salt and freshly ground pepper.

Potato Gnocchi
serves 6

Gnocchi is a light Italian dumpling made with starchy potatoes, flour, and eggs. Gnocchi is delicious served with just olive oil and Parmigiano-Reggiano or you can choose from the optional sauces listed on page 74.

INGREDIENTS

2 pounds russet potatoes
1¼ cups all-purpose flour*
½ teaspoon salt
1 teaspoon white pepper
¼ cup Parmigiano-Reggiano cheese or Pecorino Romano cheese, finely grated
2 eggs, beaten

optional sauces
Basil Pesto, Gorgonzola Sauce, Herb Butter Sauce (see page 74), Hearty Lasagna Sauce (see page 68)

PREPARATION

1. Preheat oven to 400°F. Bake potatoes until tender, about 1 hour.

2. Meanwhile, prepare a flat, clean work surface (countertop or pasta board) and line 2 sheet pans with parchment paper or clean towels.

3. Sift 1 cup of the flour into a large bowl, making a well in the center.

4. Allow the potatoes to slightly cool. Remove the skins from the potatoes. While potatoes are still warm, pass them through a potato ricer into the floured well.

5. Add the salt, white pepper, Parmigiano-Reggiano, and eggs to the well and mix using your fingertips. Knead the dough with your hands until all ingredients are incorporated. If the dough is dry then add one tablespoon of water and continue working the dough. Continue this process until the dough is easily formed into a smooth ball, about 5 minutes.

6. Divide the dough in half, and on a floured work surface, roll the first half of dough into a 1-inch-thick log; then cut into 1/2-inch-thick pieces. Lay the pieces on the sheet pans, and with the back of a fork or your thumb, make an indentation on one side. For a visual, see the photo on the next page. Refrigerate until needed. Repeat the process with the remaining dough.

7. If you are not going to cook the gnocchi immediatly, then freeze on a sheet pan.

8. In a medium stockpot, boil water. Cook gnocchi for 1-2 minutes. When they float to the surface, they are finished cooking. Remove with a slotted spoon and drain well.

9. Add desired sauce.

For a richer flavor, reduce all-purpose flour to 3/4 cup and add 1/4 cup chestnut flour.

Basil Pesto
2 cups

INGREDIENTS
2 cups basil, solidly packed
4 garlic cloves, minced
¼ cup pine nuts
¾ cup extra-virgin olive oil
½ cup Parmigiano-Reggiano cheese, freshly grated
¼ cup Pecorino Romano cheese, freshly grated

PREPARATION
1. In a food processor, blend the basil, garlic, pine nuts, and oil until smooth. Then transfer to a bowl,. Add the grated cheese and combine.

   Pesto can be stored in a glass jar topped with olive oil. Kept in the refrigerator the pesto will last for 1 week and freezes well for up to 3 months.

Gorgonzola Sauce
1½ cups

INGREDIENTS
½ stick butter or 3 tablespoons olive-oil
6 ounces Gorgonzola cheese
1 cup heavy cream
2 tablespoons Parmigiano-Reggiano cheese, freshly grated
1 teaspoon white pepper

PREPARATION
1. Melt the butter in a saucepan on low heat. Add the Gorgonzola and heavy cream. Stir until smooth.

2. Remove from heat. Add the Parmigiano-Reggiano and white pepper. Stir well.

Herb Butter Sauce
½ cup

INGREDIENTS
1 stick butter
¼ cup fresh herbs, finely chopped – a combination or one type (sage, basil, thyme, or marjoram)
1 garlic clove, finely chopped
½ teaspoon white pepper

PREPARATION
1. Melt the butter in a saucepan over low heat. Add the herbs and garlic, occasionally pressing with a spoon to extract the flavor.

2. After about 5-10 minutes, turn off heat. Remove herbs and season with white pepper.

Tomato Tart

serves 8

Delicious during late summer when tomatoes are at their peak.

INGREDIENTS

parmigiano-reggiano & pepper pastry

  1¼ cups all-purpose flour
  1 stick unsalted butter, cold, cut into ½-inch cubes
  2 tablespoons Parmigiano-Reggiano cheese, freshly grated
  ½ teaspoon black pepper
  ¼ teaspoon salt
  2-4 tablespoons ice water

filling

  ¾ pound fresh mozzarella cheese, thinly sliced
  ½ cup pesto (see recipe on page 74)
  2 pounds fresh tomatoes, sliced ½ inch thick
  10 fresh basil leaves, whole
  Salt and pepper

  special equipment: The weight of pie weights or raw rice ensures that the crust will bake flat.

PREPARATION

pastry

  1. In a large bowl, using your fingertips, blend together flour, butter, Parmigiano-Reggiano and pepper, until the mixture resembles coarse meal. Gently squeeze a small handful of the dough; if the mixture doesn't hold together, then add more water, 1 tablespoon at a time. After each addition of water, test; continue until incorporated. (Do not overwork dough.)

  2. Place the dough on a work surface and divide in half. With heel of your hand, smear each portion once in a forward motion to help distribute fat. Gather both portions of dough into a ball; then pat into a disk. Wrap in wax paper and chill until firm, about 1 hour.

  3. Using a rolling pin, on a floured surface roll out dough into a 12-inch circle. Drape the dough over a greased tart pan, then trim the excess. Lightly prick the bottom with a fork and chill until firm, about an hour.

  4. Position oven rack in the center. Preheat oven to 400°F.

  5. Line chilled shell with foil and pie weights. Bake pastry until it's golden along the rim, about 25 minutes. Carefully remove foil and weights, then allow to cool.

filling

  1. Arrange 1/3 of mozzarella in bottom of shell, spread 1/3 of the pesto, and arrange 1/3 of tomato slices. Repeat layering until all ingredients are used.

  2. Season with salt and freshly ground pepper.

Onion Tart
serves 8

This simple variation of a french savory tart which is easy to make and will indelibly impress your guests. To save time, a store-bought, unsweetened pastry crust can be used. This recipe is also delicious with the Parmigiano-Reggiano & Pepper Pastry on page 75.

INGREDIENTS

simple pastry
- 1½ cups all-purpose flour
- 1½ sticks salted butter, cold
- 1-4 tablespoons ice water

special equipment: The weight of pie weights or raw rice ensures that the crust will bake flat.

filling
- 3 tablespoons butter
- 2 pounds sweet onions, thinly sliced, then cut in half
- 4 large eggs
- 1 cup heavy cream
- ½ teaspoon grated nutmeg
- Salt and pepper

PREPARATION

pastry
1. In a large bowl, using your fingertips, blend together flour, and butter, until the mixture resembles coarse meal. Gently squeeze a small handful of the dough, if the mixture doesn't hold together, then add more water, 1 tablespoon at a time. After each addition of water, test; continue until incorporated. (Do not overwork dough.)

2. Place the dough on a work surface and divide in half. With heel of your hand, smear each portion once in a forward motion to help distribute fat. Gather both portions of dough into a ball; then pat into a disk. Wrap in wax paper or plastic wrap. Chill until firm, about 1 hour.

3. Using a rolling pin, on a floured surface roll out dough into a 12-inch circle. Drape the dough over a greased tart pan, then trim the excess. Lightly prick the bottom with a fork and chill until firm, about an hour.

4. Position oven rack in the center. Preheat oven to 400°F.

5. Line chilled shell with foil and pie weights. Bake pastry until it's golden along the rim, about 20 minutes. Carefully remove foil and weights, then allow to a cool.

filling
1. Melt butter in a sauté pan, and cook onions over medium heat, until onions are soft and golden, about 20 minutes.

2. In a large bowl, whisk together the eggs, cream, and nutmeg and then stir in the onions.

baking
1. Pour filling into tart shell, making sure onions are spread evenly. Bake until filling is set and is golden, 25 to 35 minutes.

2. Serve warm or at room temperature. Season with salt and freshly ground pepper to taste.

Margherita Pizza
makes two 12-inch thin-crust pizzas

If you desire a crispy crust, then use a pizza stone and pizza board. Be sure to purchase a large package of fresh basil, and separate the stems from the leaves. The stems will be used for making the sauce, and the leaves will be used as a fresh topping.

crust

2 teaspoons yeast or a ¼-ounce packet
1 teaspoon sugar or honey
1 cup warm water, 110-115°F
2¾ cups all-purpose flour
¼ cup semolina
½ teaspoon salt
1-2 tablespoons extra-virgin olive oil
¼ cup cornmeal, for the pizza stone

1. Add yeast and sweetener to warm water. Set aside for 5 to 10 minutes, until foamy.

2. Using a mixer with a dough hook, add the flour, semolina and salt to your bowl. On low speed, slowly add liquid mixture. Leave on low speed for 3-5 minutes, incorporating dough into a smooth ball. If dough is dry, then add more water. If you don't own a mixer, mix and knead by hand.

3. Remove the dough from the bowl and coat with olive oil; place dough back into the bowl. Cover with a towel and set aside in a warm place for 1 hour or until the dough has doubled in size.

tomato sauce

¼ cup extra-virgin olive oil
1 onion, diced
1 carrot, cut into ½ inch rounds
4 garlic cloves, finely minced
1 32-ounce can diced tomatoes with basil
¾ cup mushrooms, sliced
1 tablespoon oregano, chopped
1 tablespoon basil, chopped
6 basil stems (remove the leaves and reserve for topping)
½ teaspoon dried red pepper flakes
1 tablespoon balsamic vinegar
Salt and pepper

1. Preheat sauté pan on medium heat; add olive oil. Add onion, carrot, and garlic; sauté until onions are translucent.

2. Add tomatoes, mushrooms, oregano, basil and stems, red pepper, balsamic vinegar, salt, and freshly ground pepper to taste.

3. Cook sauce over high heat for 2 minutes; then simmer for 1 hour. When sauce is finished, remove basil stems. For a smooth sauce, purée in a food processor or blender.

toppings

1 cup mozzarella cheese, sliced
1 cup chèvre goat cheese or feta cheese
1 tomato, thinly sliced
½ red onion, thinly sliced
½ cup basil leaves, chopped

assembly

1. Place pizza stone in the oven. Preheat oven to 450°F for 45 minutes. Coat pizza stone with cornmeal; this will ensure that the pizza will be easily removed from the oven. If you don't own a pizza stone, use a pizza pan.

2. On a floured work surface, roll out half of the dough to the size of your pizza stone or pan. Then sprinkle the cornmeal on the pizza board and place the dough on the board. Cornmeal makes transferring pizza from board to oven easier. If you're using a pizza pan, transfer the dough to the pan.

3. Coat pizza dough with half the red sauce, half the cheese, and half the toppings.

4. Bake for 10-15 minutes, depending on desired crispness.

5. Once the pizza has been removed from the oven, add half of the chopped basil.

6. Repeat the same process for the second pizza.

Arugula & Prosciutto Pizza
— makes two 12-inch thin-crust pizzas —

This pizza is an elaborate variation on traditional pizza. It's a white pizza, meaning it doesn't have red sauce, has minimal cheese, but is nonetheless rich with many other flavors. Fresh mozzarella or chèvre goat cheese can be used instead of Parmigiano-Reggiano.

INGREDIENTS
Pizza dough (see recipe on page 79)
2 cups Parmigiano-Reggiano cheese, freshly grated
¼ cup balsamic vinegar
¼ cup extra-virgin olive oil
12 fresh figs, cut into wedges (optional)
20 slices of prosciutto
6 cups of arugula
Salt and pepper
¼ cup cornmeal

PREPARATION
1. Place pizza stone in the oven. Preheat oven to 400°F for 45 minutes. Coat pizza stone with cornmeal. This will ensure that the pizza will be easily removed from the oven. If you don't own a pizza stone, use a pizza pan.

2. Roll out half of the dough on a floured work surface, to the size of your pizza stone or pan. Then add the cornmeal to the pizza board and place the dough on the board. If you're using a pizza pan, transfer the dough to the pan. Cornmeal makes transferring pizza from board to oven easier.

3. Brush on a light coat of oil, and sprinkle 1/2 cup of the Parmigiano-Reggiano over the dough.

4. Bake pizza until crust is golden brown, about 10-15 minutes.

5. Meanwhile, in a medium bowl, add the vinegar and oil. Set dressing aside.

6. Take pizza crust out of the oven. Drape half of the prosciutto slices over pizza, covering completely. Arrange half of the fig wedges on the pizza.

7. Put back into the oven and bake until figs are warm and soft, about 2-3 minutes. Transfer pizza to cutting board.

8. In a large bowl, add half the arugula and mix with half the oil-and-vinegar dressing. Mound arugula on top of the pizza crust. Sprinkle another 1/2 cup of Parmigiano-Reggiano over salad. Add salt and freshly ground pepper to taste.

9. Repeat same process for second pizza.

Grilled Cheese Sandwich
~ serves 6 ~

The ultimate comfort food; Smoked Gouda and Gruyère grilled cheese, topped with prosciutto, caramelized onions, and arugula perfectly pairs with hot tomato soup (see recipe is on page 61.)

INGREDIENTS
1 loaf of country style bread, cut into 12 pieces ½ inch thick
Herb Butter Sauce using sage (see recipe on page 74)
8 ounces Gouda cheese, grated
8 ounces Gruyère cheese, grated
½ pound prosciutto
1 cup caramelized onions (see recipe below)
1 cup arugula

PREPARATION
1. Arrange the bread slices on a work surface. Brush both sides of the bread with melted Herb Butter Sauce. Add grated cheese to 6 bread slices, and then add the prosciutto. Top with remaining 6 bread slices.

2. Heat a large skillet or grill pan over medium heat. Place sandwiches on the skillet and cook until golden brown on bottom, about 4 to 5 minutes. Then turn sandwiches over and do the same until the cheese melts, approximately 4 minutes more. Open each sandwich, add a spoonful of caramelized onions and a few leaves of arugula.

Caramelized Onions
~ 1 cup ~

INGREDIENTS
2 medium sweet onions
2 teaspoons olive oil
1 tablespoons white vinegar
Salt to taste

PREPARATION
1. Slice off the root and top ends of the onions, then peel. Cut the onions in half, then thinly slice crosswise leaving ringlets.

2. Use a large sauté pan, heat the oil on medium high heat until hot. Add the onion rings and vinegar. Stir to coat.

3. Reduce heat to low and allow onions to cook for 45 to 60 minutes, stirring every few minutes allowing onions to brown. If you stir them too often, they won't brown. Add salt and pepper to taste.

4. Store refrigerated in an air tight container for several days.

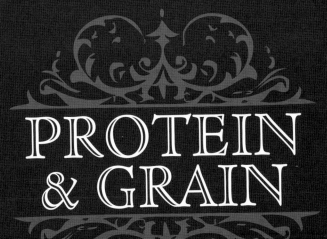

PROTEIN & GRAIN

CHAPTER

No. 7

Duck & Mushroom Risotto
Quinoa Garlic Greens
Lamb Chops with Polenta
Grilled Pork Tenderloin
Salmon or Whitefish with Citrus Marinade
Barbecue Buffalo Burgers with Baked Beans
Barbecue Chicken
Stuffed Poblano Peppers

Duck & Mushroom Risotto
— serves 6 —

This is a great recipe for using leftover poultry. Instead of using duck, you can substitute the dark meat from a turkey or chicken. A vegetarian version is also delicious and is made by replacing the chicken stock with vegetable stock and omitting the poultry.

INGREDIENTS
2 cups dry red wine
4–6 cups chicken or vegetable stock
4 tablespoons butter
1½ cups onions, chopped
2 tablespoons garlic, finely chopped
1 teaspoon thyme, finely chopped
1 teaspoon oregano, finely chopped
3 cups mushrooms – oyster, shiitake, and crimini, coarsely chopped
1½ cups arborio rice
2 cups duck, chicken, or turkey meat, cooked and shredded
1 cup Parmigiano-Reggiano cheese, finely grated
Salt and pepper

PREPARATION
1. In a small saucepan, over medium heat, reduce wine in half (from two cups to one). This creates an intensely flavored wine reduction.

2. In a stockpot, add stock and simmer. Cover to keep warm.

3. In a large sauté pan, melt the butter over medium heat. Add the onions, garlic, thyme, and oregano. Sauté for 1 minute. Add the mushrooms and sauté for about 3 minutes.

4. Add the dry rice to the onion mixture, stirring constantly to coat, about 2 minutes or until opaque. Add the wine and stir until the liquid is absorbed.

5. Add 1 cup of the hot stock, stirring constantly until all the liquid is absorbed. Continue adding 1/2 cup stock and stirring until absorbed and continue this process until the consistency is smooth and creamy. This should take about 30-40 minutes.

6. Fold in the duck and stir. Then fold in the Parmigiano-Reggiano and mix well.

7. Season with salt and freshly ground pepper to taste.

Quinoa & Garlic Greens
with sausage
serves 6

Quinoa is highly appreciated for its nutritional value. It has a high protein content, as well as being high in phosphorus, magnesium, and iron. Quinoa is gluten-free. For a vegetarian meal, omit the sausage and use vegetable stock.

INGREDIENTS

1 cup quinoa
2 cups chicken or vegetable stock
2 tablespoons olive oil
1 pound chicken sausage links, sliced crosswise
¾ cup chopped onion
3-6 large cloves of garlic, minced
6-8 cups chopped fresh dark greens (spinach, kale, or chard)
½ teaspoon red pepper flakes
3 tablespoons pine nuts
⅓ cup Pecorino Romano cheese, grated

PREPARATION

1. Soak the quinoa in water in a fine mesh strainer for thirty minutes. Rinse and drain well.

2. In a stockpot over high heat, add the stock and bring to a boil. Add the quinoa, then lower heat and simmer for approximately 15 minutes. Remove quinoa from heat, cover, and allow to rest for 5 minutes. Gently fluff with a fork.

3. In a sauté pan, heat 1 tablespoon of the olive oil over medium high heat. Sauté sausages until cooked. Pre-cooked sausages should cook for 3-4 minutes per side; fresh sausages should cook for 5-9 minutes per side.

4. Meanwhile, in a large saute pan over medium heat, add 1 tablespoon of the olive oil. Sauté onions and garlic until translucent, approximately 5 minutes. Add the fresh greens and red pepper flakes. Sauté for 3-4 minutes, until greens are lightly wilted.

5. Serve the quinoa in large bowls, and top with greens and sausage mixture. Sprinkle pine nuts and Pecorino Romano over each dish and serve immediately.

Contributor: Monica Verplank

Lamb Chops
with polenta
— serves 6 —

INGREDIENTS

polenta
- 1¼ cups polenta
- 4 cups of chicken or vegetable stock
- 1 tbsp olive oil
- 3 garlic cloves, minced
- ½ cup sweet onion, minced (optional)
- 1 teaspoon fresh rosemary, minced

PREPARATION

1. In a large saucepan, heat the stock over medium heat. In a sauté pan, add the olive oil, garlic, sweet onion and rosemary. Sauté until the onions become translucent, about 5 minutes.

2. Stir the polenta, garlic, and onion mixture into the hot stock. Continue constantly stirring until the polenta thickens and begins to pull away from the sides of the pan, about 25-35 minutes.

3. Immediately pour the polenta onto an oiled sheet pan or plate and flatten to about 1/2 to 3/4 of an inch. Refrigerate until firm, then cut as desired and grill. Cookie cutters can create fun polenta shapes!

4. Grill polenta until it is golden brown, about 3 minutes per side.

fresh herb rub
- 4 large garlic cloves, crushed
- 1 tablespoon fresh rosemary leaves
- 1 tablespoon fresh basil
- 1 tablespoon fresh parsley
- 1 lemon, juiced
- 2 tablespoons extra-virgin olive oil
- 1 teaspoon coarse sea salt

lamb
- 12 lamb chops, about ¾ inch thick

PREPARATION

1. In a food processor or blender, add all of the herb rub ingredients and pulse to combine into a paste. Rub on both sides of the lamb chops. Refrigerate for a least 1 hour before cooking. Preheat the grill or stovetop. Use the directions below according to your cooking method.

2. *Grill:* Preheat the grill on high for 10 minutes, then reduce to medium heat. Grill the lamb chops, 2 to 4 minutes per side for medium-rare.

3. *Stovetop:* Preheat the grill pan on medium heat. Grill the lamb chops, 2 to 4 minutes per side for medium-rare.

4. Remove from heat, transfer lamb to a platter, and serve.

Grilled Pork Tenderloin
with grilled asparagus
serves 6

INGREDIENTS

2 pounds pork tenderloin
6 garlic cloves, peeled and halved
2 tablespoons olive oil
1 pound asparagus
kitchen string

spicy rub

2 teaspoons red pepper flakes, crushed
½ teaspoon onion powder
½ teaspoon celery salt
½ teaspoon ground cumin
½ teaspoon white pepper
¼ teaspoon cayenne pepper
½ teaspoon paprika
½ teaspoon dill weed
1 teaspoon coarse sea salt

PREPARATION

1. Slice pork tenderloin lengthwise, approximately 1 inch deep. Do not slice all the way through the meat.

2. Insert the garlic directly into the slice, laying cloves end to end. Rub exterior of meat with 1 tablespoon of the olive oil. Then tie the pork tenderloin together with kitchen string.

3. Mix all ingredients for the spice rub in a jar with a removable lid.

4. Sprinkle two tablespoons or more spice mixture onto the exterior of the tenderloin. Use a spoon or rubber gloves to rub the seasoning into the meat. The mixture includes crushed red pepper flakes; therefore, avoid excessive contact with your skin.

5. Allow the meat to rest for thirty minutes in the refrigerator.

6. Preheat the grill on medium high.

7. Toss the asparagus in olive oil and set aside.

8. Grill tenderloin over medium heat for 7-10 minutes per side. Add asparagus to the grill when turning the tenderloin over. For safety, the USDA recommends cooking pork to 160°F.

9. When finished cooking, cover the tenderloin with aluminium foil and allow to rest for 3-5 minutes. Use a kitchen knife to remove the string before slicing.

Contributor: Monica Verplank

Salmon or Whitefish with Citrus Marinade
serves 6

A versatile marinade for most meat, poultry, or fish. Perfect for both sautéing and grilling.

INGREDIENTS

citrus marinade
½ cup fresh lemon, lime or orange juice
5 garlic cloves, minced
½ teaspoon chipotle pepper flakes
½ teaspoon coarsely ground black pepper
½ cup extra-virgin olive oil
¼ cup fresh herbs, coarsely chopped (basil, cilantro, dill, parsley, or a mixture)

fish & greens
6 fish fillets, 4-6-ounces each
6 ounces fresh spinach or arugula

PREPARATION

1. Use a glass jar with a screw top that holds a minimum of 16 ounces. Combine the citrus juice, garlic, chipotle flakes, and coarsely ground black pepper. Add olive oil and herbs, and shake well. This can be made a day ahead for better flavor.

2. Using half of the marinade, marinate the fish for thirty minutes. Reserve the remainder for the dressing.

3. Preheat the grill or stovetop using medium heat. Use the directions below according to your cooking method.

4. *Grill:* Place the fish on the cooking grate and grill (salmon 6-8 minutes, whitefish 5 minutes) on each side or until the fish is opaque but still moist in thickest part.

5. *Stovetop:* In a large sauté pan, heat one tablespoon olive oil, and sauté (salmon 6-8 minutes, whitefish 5 minutes) on each side or until the fish is opaque but still moist in thickest part.

6. Prepare plates by adding about an ounce (a small handful) of spinach or arugula to the center of each plate. Remove the skin and place the fish on top of the greens. Use the reserved marinade as a dressing.

Barbecue Buffalo Burgers

⟶ serves 6 ⟵

Buffalo is a delicious lean alternative to beef. It's extremely high in iron and vitamins. Because buffalo is lower in fat than ground beef, it should be cooked slowly and at a lower temperature.

burgers
barbecue sauce (see recipe on page 98)
1½ pounds ground buffalo
1 tablespoon butter
6 onion rolls, cut lengthwise

garnish
1 cup caramelized onions (see recipe on page 83)
4 ounces goat cheese or Gorgonzola cheese
4 ounces arugula

PREPARATION

1. Divide ground buffalo into six even portions and shape into 1/2-inch patties. Marinate burgers in barbecue sauce for 30 minutes before cooking.

2. Preheat the grill or stovetop using medium heat. Use the directions below according to your cooking method.

3. *Grill:* Grill the buffalo patties for 7-9 minutes. Using a spatula, turn burgers over once or twice. Once the burgers are almost cooked, grill the onion rolls, turning over once with tongs until toasted, about 2 minutes total.

4. *Stovetop:* Heat the butter in a large sauté pan. Cook the buffalo patties for 7-9 minutes. Turn burgers over once or twice. Once the burgers are almost cooked, put the onion rolls under the broiler, turning over once with tongs until toasted, about 2 minutes total.

5. Serve burgers on the warm rolls, slather with extra barbecue sauce and garnish with arugula, caramelized onions, and a dollop of goat cheese.

Michigan Baked Beans

⟶ serves 8 ⟵

bean preparation
3 cups pinto beans, dry*
2 garlic cloves, whole
¼ onion, whole
1 bay leaf

baked beans
¾ cup ketchup
¼ cup mustard
2 cups onion, chopped
4 tablespoons vinegar
⅛ cup Michigan maple syrup
½ pound bacon, partially cooked, cut in bite-sized pieces

PREPARATION

1. Soak the pinto beans overnight in a large pot of water, approximately 9 cups.

2. Drain and rinse the beans and replace with fresh water, covering the beans by 2 inches. Add garlic, 1/4 onion, and a bay leaf. Bring to a rapid boil, then simmer covered for about 1 hour, adding more water if necessary. When beans have reached desired tenderness, drain and rinse again. Remove the garlic, the onion and the bay leaf.

3. Preheat oven to 350°F.

4. In an 8" x 10" pan, mix beans with remaining ingredients. Cover and bake for 2½ to 3 hours.

   *Pinto beans will expand two to three times in size; one cup of dried beans will equal between 2-3 cups of cooked beans. Fresh beans (1 to 3 years old) need less time to soak and cook.

Barbecue Chicken
serves 6

INGREDIENTS
6 chicken breasts, 4-6 ounces each
¾ cup barbecue sauce (see recipe below)
2 tablespoons extra-virgin olive oil

PREPARATION

1. Marinate the chicken breasts in barbecue sauce for thirty minutes.

2. Preheat the grill or stovetop using medium heat. Use the directions below according to your cooking method.

3. *Grill:* Using the grill, place the chicken on the cooking grate and grill for 8-10 minutes on each side. For safety, the USDA recommends cooking chicken to 165°F.

4. *Stovetop:* Using a large sauté pan, heat one tablespoon olive oil, and sauté the chicken for 8-10 minutes on each side. Serve hot. For safety, the USDA recommends cooking chicken to 165°F.

Barbecue Sauce
1 1/2 cups

Barbecue sauce is a delicious addition to a burger, chicken breast, or pork loin.

INGREDIENTS
1 cup ketchup
3 tablespoons molasses
¼ cup white vinegar
3 tablespoons Worcestershire sauce
2 tablespoons Dijon mustard
¼ cup whiskey
2 tablespoons fresh lemon juice
¼ teaspoon cayenne
1½ teaspoons onion powder
1½ teaspoons garlic powder
½ teaspoon chili powder
½ teaspoon white pepper
1 teaspoon ground cumin

PREPARATION

1. Make barbecue sauce a day ahead.

2. Use a glass jar with a removable lid; add all the ingredients and shake well.

3. Refrigerate the sauce; it will last up to a week.

Stuffed Poblano Peppers
serves 6

INGREDIENTS

2 pounds boneless chuck roast
8 garlic cloves, whole
1 tablespoon extra-virgin olive oil
2 tablespoons flour
½ onion, diced
3 jalapeños, seeded and diced
1 cup water
2 bay leaves
2 tablespoons Dijon mustard
15 peppercorns
1 teaspoon salt
10-12 poblano peppers
2 cups cheddar cheese, grated

PREPARATION

1. Pierce 8 holes into the boneless chuck roast, and push one garlic clove into each hole. Spread olive oil evenly across the surface of the meat.

2. Dust both sides of meat lightly with flour.

3. Using a large sauté pan, heat the olive oil over high heat and brown meat on both sides.

4. Transfer the meat to a crock pot. Add the onion, jalapeños, water, bay leaves, mustard, peppercorns and salt. Set crock pot to low and cook slowly for 5-6 hours.

5. Cut the poblano peppers in half lengthwise, remove the seeds and ribs.

6. Fill each pepper with cooked meat, top with cheese, and broil for 5-6 minutes, watching for peppers to brown and cheese to melt.

7. For a complete meal, serve with a grain such as rice and a salad.

Contributor: Monica Verplank

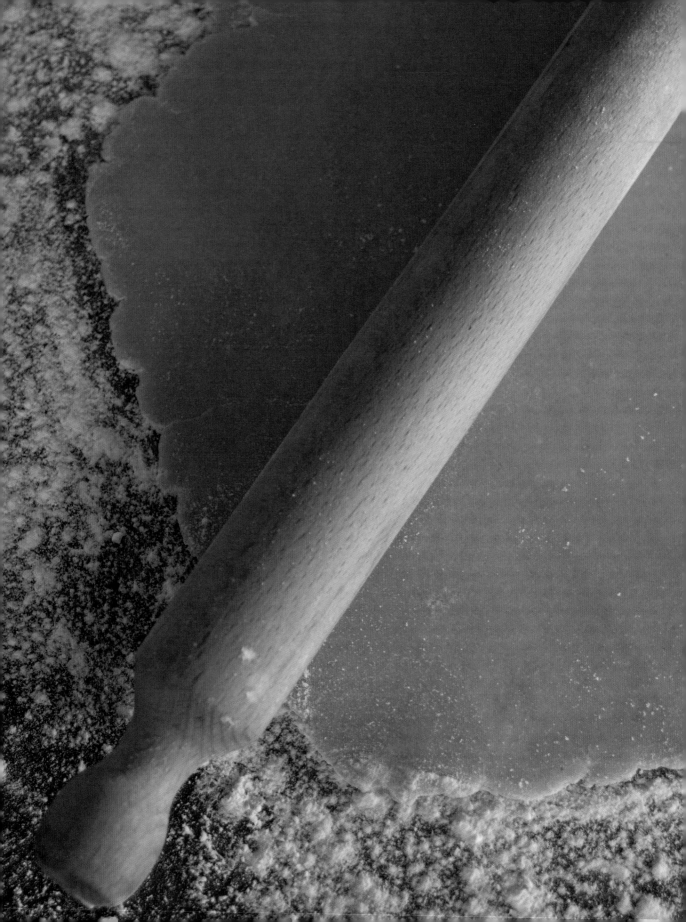

SWEETS

CHAPTER
No. 7

Oatmeal Chocolate Chip Cookies
~ 24 cookies ~

Oatmeal cookies are natural power bars, and are great to take along when hiking, biking or skiing.

INGREDIENTS
2 sticks salted butter, at room temperature for 1 hour to soften
1 cup light-brown sugar
2 eggs
1 tablespoon vanilla
½ teaspoon baking soda
1 cup all-purpose flour
2 cups oats
1 cup unsweetened coconut, finely shredded
12 ounces dark chocolate chips
¾ cup almonds, chestnuts, or walnuts, toasted, cooled, and chopped

PREPARATION
1. Preheat oven to 350°F. Lightly butter two cookie sheets, or use a silicone or parchment liner.

2. In a large bowl, mix together the softened butter and sugar.

3. Add eggs, vanilla and baking soda, then mix until incorporated. Stir in flour, oats, coconut, chocolate, and nuts.

4. On a sheet pan, arrange 1/4 cup mounds of cookie dough, about 12 cookies per sheet. Then gently flatten each mound of dough to about 1/2-inch thick.

5. Bake in the center of oven, rotating pans halfway through, until golden, about 12-15 minutes.

6. Remove from the oven. With a spatula, transfer to cooling racks to cool completely.

Flourless Chocolate Cake
serves 20

A chocolate-lover's dream, an intensely flavored chocolate cake with two delicious seasonal sauces: fresh raspberries in the summer, and freshly whipped cream in the winter.

INGREDIENTS

cake
- 6 ounces semisweet chocolate
- 6 ounces dark or bittersweet chocolate
- 1 pound unsalted butter, diced
- 1 cup freshly brewed espresso
- 1 cup brown sugar
- 8 large eggs, beaten

ganache
- 8 ounces semisweet chocolate, cut into small pieces
- ½ cup heavy whipping cream
- 2 tablespoons unsalted butter

sauce
- 3 pints of fresh ripe raspberries (summer)
- 2 cups of heavy cream (winter)
- 1 tablespoon powdered sugar

CAKE

1. Preheat the oven to 350°F. Line the bottom of a round 9-inch cake pan (2-inches deep) with parchment. Place the chocolate in a large bowl. Bring the butter, espresso, and sugar to boil in a medium saucepan, stirring to dissolve the sugar. Add the hot mixture to the chocolate and whisk until smooth. Whisk in the eggs and pour the batter into the pan.

2. Next, make a hot water bath by placing the cake pan into a roasting pan. Place in the oven. Pour hot water into the roasting pan to come halfway up sides of cake pan, about 1 inch. Bake until cake is set, and the center is firm, about 1 hour. Remove the pan from oven. Chill cake.

3. To loosen cake, cut around sides of pan and place flat dish over pan, hold pan and platter together tightly and invert. Remove cake pan and peel off parchment.

GANACHE

1. To make the ganache, place the chopped chocolate in a medium-sized stainless steel bowl and set aside. Heat the cream and butter in a medium saucepan over medium heat and bring to a boil. Pour the hot cream over the chocolate and allow it to melt for a few minutes, then stir with a whisk to incorporate.

2. Place the cake on a wire rack on top of a sheet pan. This way, if the ganache drips it will end up on the sheet pan, which makes cleanup easier. Using a cake spatula, cover the sides and top of the cake with about 4 tablespoons ganache. This is a crumb coat which seals in any loose crumbs so your cake will have a smooth finish. Refrigerate cake for 5 minutes for crumb coat to set.

3. Add another layer of ganache. Pour the remaining ganache onto the center of the cake. Using a spatula, using big strokes to smooth ganache over the top and then the sides of the cake.

4. Serve with raspberry sauce and fresh berries, or freshly whipped cream.

SAUCE

1. *Raspberry Sauce:* Working in batches, purée half of raspberries in a blender. To remove the seeds, strain the purée, pour into a container and chill. This can be made a day in advance.

2. *Whipped Cream:* Pour the cream and sugar into a bowl, stirring to dissolve sugar. Whip the cream by hand or with a mixer on high speed until peaks form. Don't overmix.

Fudgy Cashew Butter Brownies
∽ serves 12 ∾

This updated classic consists of three layers: a dense brownie center, a creamy cashew butter coating, and finally, a smooth layer of ganache topped with crunchy nuts.

INGREDIENTS

brownies
- 2 sticks butter, unsalted
- 6 ounces semisweet chocolate
- 6 ounces dark chocolate
- 1¼ cups sugar
- 1 tablespoon vanilla extract
- ¼ teaspoon salt
- 4 eggs, beaten
- 1¼ cups all purpose flour
- 1 cup salted cashews, hazelnuts, or peanuts, chopped

frosting
- 1½ cups nut butter (cashew, hazelnut, or peanut)
- ¼ cup butter, unsalted, at room temperature for 1 hour to soften
- ⅛ teaspoon salt
- ⅛ teaspoon ground nutmeg
- 1 teaspoon vanilla extract

ganache
- Ganache (see recipe on page 105)

PREPARATION

brownies
1. Position the rack in the center of oven, and preheat to 325°F. Use a 13 x 9 x 2-inch nonstick sheet pan, and coat with butter.

2. In a large saucepan, melt butter and chocolates and stir over very low heat until smooth. Remove from heat and incorporate the sugar, vanilla, and salt. Once blended, add the eggs, fold in the flour, and then add the nuts.

3. Spread into prepared pan. Bake for about 30 minutes until firm to the touch. Place pan onto a cooling rack.

frosting
1. Using a mixer, beat the nut butter and butter together and then add salt, nutmeg, and vanilla.

2. Spread frosting over brownies and refrigerate.

ganache
1. Cut brownies into squares, bars, or triangles. This can be done before or after the ganache application. Cutting the brownies after the ganache application will showcase the layers.

2. To coat with ganache, place brownies on a wire rack on top of a sheet pan. This way, if the ganache drips it will end up on the sheet pan, which makes cleanup easier. Pour ganache over cashew butter frosting and spread to cover. Do this quickly before the ganache sets. Refrigerate until firm, about 1 hour. Top with salted nuts.

Minty Fruit Salad
serves 8

Fresh fruit is at its seasonal peak during the summer months, but this salad can be made any time of the year with any combination of fruit. To sweeten further, add honey or maple syrup.

INGREDIENTS
1 cup blackberries
1 cup blueberries
1 cups cantaloupe, cut into ¾-inch squares
1 cup nectarines, cut into thin wedges
1 cup strawberries, cut into halves
1 cup sweet cherries, cut in half and pitted
¼ cup fresh mint, finely chopped
2 limes, juiced
2 tablespoons honey or maple syrup (optional)

PREPARATION
1. In a mixing bowl, combine the fruit, mint, lime juice; and gently toss. If your fruit isn't sweet enough, then drizzle it with honey or maple syrup.

2. Serve in parfait dishes or small bowls.

Pear & Basil Salad
serves 6

Pears and grapes paired with honey, balsamic, basil, and Parmesan make a light but savory dessert. Pears and grapes peak in late summer, early fall.

INGREDIENTS
4 pears, cored and cut into 8 wedges
1 cup seedless grapes, cut in half
1 teaspoon honey
2 tablespoons extra-virgin olive oil
1 tablespoons balsamic vinegar
¼ cup Parmigiano-Reggiano shavings
¼ cup fresh basil leaves, finely chopped

PREPARATION
1. In a medium bowl, add pears and grapes. In a glass jar with a removable lid, add the honey, oil, and vinegar, and shake well. Pour mixture over pear and grape salad, and toss to coat.

2. Arrange the pears on a serving platter. Sprinkle with cheese shavings and chopped basil.

Note: To create Parmesan shavings, draw a vegetable peeler across a wedge of cheese.

Sweet Pastry
makes 2 tart crusts

A classic sweet pastry provides a stable crust that is excellent for fruit pies and tarts.

INGREDIENTS
1 stick butter, unsalted
2½ cups all-purpose flour
⅛ teaspoon salt
½ cup sugar
2 eggs
1 teaspoon vanilla

special equipment: pie weights or raw rice

PREPARATION
1. Remove butter from the refrigerator an hour beforehand to soften. Consistency should be cool yet malleable.

2. In a medium bowl, add flour, salt, and sugar. In another bowl, mix together the butter, eggs, and vanilla until smooth. Then combine both mixtures.

3. With your fingertips, knead dough until it comes together in moist clumps. If dough is too dry, add a few drops of water and incorporate. Gather dough into ball; divide in half and flatten into two disks. Wrap in wax paper and chill until firm, at least 1 hour. Freeze half the dough for later use.

4. Position rack in center of oven; preheat to 400°F. On a floured work surface, roll out the dough to a 10-inch circle. Carefully transfer dough to 9-inch greased tart pan with a removable bottom. Gently press dough up the sides of pan, pressing to adhere. Trim excess dough from sides of pan.

5. Line crust with foil, and fill with rice or pie weights. Bake sweet pastry until sides of crust are set, about 20 minutes.

6. Remove from oven and cool in pan on wire rack. Remove foil and pie weights. Leave the sweet pastry in the pan; it's now ready for use.

Pear Tart
serves 8

Holiday guests will be impressed with this simple yet elegant dessert.

INGREDIENTS
2 pounds pears, preferably Bosc
1 lemon, juiced
½ stick unsalted butter
⅓ cup sugar
¼ teaspoon cinnamon

sweet pastry
Sweet pastry crust (see recipe on page 110)

PREPARATION
1. Preheat the oven to 425°F.

2. To prepare the filling, peel the pears; core and cut them into 1/4-inch slices. In a large bowl, toss the pear slices with the lemon juice (this prevents browning).

3. In a large sauté pan, melt butter over moderate heat until the foam subsides. Then stir in sugar (the sugar will not dissolve until the pears are added). Add the pears, sprinkle with cinnamon, and sauté until sugar turns a deep golden caramel. Allow pears to cool completely.

4. Lay the slices in an overlapping, fanned pattern until the entire tart is covered. Use the smaller pear slices to create a rosette or pattern in the center. Pour the remaining sauce over pears.

5. Bake the tart for 15 minutes at 425°F. Then reduce the oven temperature to 350°F and bake for another 20 minutes, until the pears are tender and the crust is golden brown.

6. Remove from oven, and allow to cool for 1 hour. Remove from pan and serve.

Blueberry Galette
two medium tarts

The summer of 2010 was an epic wild berry season in Michigan's upper peninsula; blueberries, bilberries and huckleberries blanketed to landscape. I highly recommended using wild berries because the flavor is much more intense. When using domestic berries, you may need to add more sweetener. Serve with freshly whipped cream or vanilla ice cream.

INGREDIENTS

galette dough
½ cup water, cold
2 tablespoons honey
2½ cups all-purpose flour
1 stick butter, cold, cut into ½-inch cubes

filling
4 -5 cups blueberries
½ cup honey, add more for desired sweetness
1 lemon, juiced
1/2 teaspoon vanilla*

egg wash
1 large egg yolk
1 tablespoon milk

PREPARATION

1. Add the honey to the water.

2. In a large bowl, using your fingertips, blend together flour, butter, and 1/4 cup of water and honey mixture, until it resembles coarse meal. Gently squeeze together a small handful of dough, if the mixture doesn't hold together, then add more water, 1 tablespoon at a time. After each addition of water, test; continue until incorporated. (Do not overwork dough.)

3. Place the dough on a work surface and divide in half. With heel of your hand, smear each portion once in a forward motion to help distribute fat. Gather both portions of dough and shape into two disks. Wrap in wax paper and chill until firm, about 1 hour.

4. Position oven rack in the center. Preheat oven to 400°F.

5. In a bowl add the blueberries, honey, lemon, and vanilla*. Mix Gently.

6. Remove dough from refrigerator and roll each half disc into an 11" circle, about 1/8-inch thick. Move dough to a sheet pan. Mound 2 cups of the blueberry mixture in middle of each circle, leaving a border of about 2 inches. Fold in the borders to partially cover the fruit.

7. Whisk together the egg and the milk, then brush over the dough. Bake for 50 minutes, until crust is golden. Allow to cool and enjoy.

Use vanilla with domestic berries.

Zucchini Bread
— two mini-loaves or 16 muffins —

This recipe presents a twist on traditional zucchini bread by adding carrots, chocolate, oats, and chestnuts.

INGREDIENTS

1 tablespoon unsalted butter
1 stick unsalted butter, melted
½ cup applesauce
1 cup honey
½ teaspoon vanilla
4 large eggs
3 cups unbleached all-purpose flour
2 teaspoons baking powder
½ tablespoon baking soda
⅛ teaspoon nutmeg
⅛ teaspoon salt
½ cup shredded carrots
1½ cup shredded zucchini
⅓ cup dark chocolate chips
⅓ cup chestnuts, finely chopped*
⅓ cup oats

PREPARATION

1. Preheat the oven to 350°F. Use either a muffin pan or mini loaf pans. Grease pans with 1 or 2 teaspoon of butter.

2. In a large bowl, combine wet ingredients: the melted butter, applesauce, honey, vanilla and eggs. Hand mix until incorporated.

3. Sift the dry ingredients together: flour, baking powder, baking soda, nutmeg, and salt. Add the dry ingredients to the wet ingredients, and hand mix until all the ingredients are incorporated, and the batter is smooth.

4. Fold in the shredded carrots, zucchini, dark chocolate chips, chestnuts, and oats.

5. Pour the batter into the prepared pans and bake. Bake until golden brown; muffins usually need 35 minutes, mini loaves 45 minutes, and a regular loaf 1 hour. The bread is finished when a skewer or toothpick is inserted in the center and comes out clean, without crumbs attached.

6. Remove from the oven and allow to cool for 10 minutes before serving.

If you can't find fresh chestnuts then use peeled frozen chestnuts or dried chestnut slices. Follow the directions on the packaging for preparation.

Plum or Cherry Granita
serves 8

Granita is a frozen dessert made from sugar, water, and flavorings. No specialized equipment is needed to make granita. Simply pour the fruit mixture into a shallow pan, place in your freezer, and stir every 45 minutes until mixture is frozen and grainy.

INGREDIENTS

2 cups water
½ -1 cup sugar or honey
1 lemon, freshly squeezed
¼ teaspoon vanilla extract
3 pounds plums or sweet cherries

PREPARATION

1. In a saucepan, combine the water, sugar, lemon juice and vanilla extract. Bring to a simmer, and stir until the sugar is dissolved. Refrigerate the simple syrup.

2. Remove the pits from the fruit and mash with a fork. In a blender or food processor, purée the fruit with the simple syrup until smooth. Refrigerate at least 4 hours to allow the flavors to blend. Then pour into a shallow, freezer-safe container and freeze.

3. After 45 minutes, stir and scrape the mixture using a rubber spatula. Again, freeze for 45 minutes, then stir and scrape, using a fork as it thickens. Continue every 45 minutes until mixture is grainy. This process should take 3-4 hours. Serve in chilled bowls.

Roasted Pears or Apples
serves 6

INGREDIENTS

3 tablespoons unsalted butter
¼ cup honey
½ teaspoon vanilla extract
4 large pears or apples, quartered lengthwise, and cored
½ cup chestnuts, boiled or roasted then peeled and chopped

serve with
Vanilla ice cream or
Naturally Sweetened Ricotta (see recipe on page 124)

PREPARATION

1. Preheat the oven to 350°F.

2. In an ovenproof skillet on medium heat, melt the butter; add honey and vanilla. Then add the pears or apples, and chestnuts. Sauté for 5 minutes, turning frequently to coat with sauce.

3. Transfer pan to oven, and roast in oven for 15 minutes.

4. Serve warm with vanilla ice cream or Naturally Sweetened Ricotta, see recipe page 124.

Homemade Ricotta
2-3 cups

In Italian, ricotta means twice cooked. Traditionally, ricotta is produced from whey, the liquid that is separated from the curds when cheese is made. When making ricotta for dessert, use lemon juice and omit the salt.

INGREDIENTS
1 gallon whole milk (cow, goat, or sheep)
½ teaspoon salt (optional)
⅓ cup fresh lemon juice or white vinegar

special equipment: large sieve, fine-mesh cheesecloth

PREPARATION
1. Line a large sieve with a layer of cheesecloth, and place it over a large bowl.

2. Slowly bring milk and the optional salt to a rolling boil in a 6-quart heavy pot over moderate heat. Stir occasionally to prevent scorching. Reduce heat to a simmer.

3. Add lemon juice or vinegar, and stir gently. Allow to rest for 10 minutes. Spoon the curds into a cheesecloth-lined sieve, and let it drain 1 hour. After discarding the liquid, cover and chill the ricotta. Store covered in the refrigerator for 1-2 weeks.

Chocolate Ricotta Mousse
serves 4

INGREDIENTS
4 ounces semisweet chocolate
4 ounces bittersweet chocolate
¾ cup whipping cream
2 cups ricotta, recipe above
2 tablespoons powdered sugar
1 teaspoon vanilla extract

garnish
1 cup any fresh fruit or marinated berries (see recipe on page 124)
¼ cup semisweet or dark chocolate, chopped

PREPARATION
1. Warm the chocolate and the cream over low heat until melted.

2. Blend the ricotta, sugar, and vanilla in a food processor until smooth and then mix the warm chocolate into the mixture. Refrigerate for at least 1 hour. Can be frozen as well.

3. Garnish with fresh or marinated berries, fruit, and/or shaved chocolate.

Pecan Carmel Tart
serves 8

The rich pecans and sweet caramel provide a delightful filling for this hearty tart.

INGREDIENTS
1½ cups heavy cream
¼ cup water
⅓ cup honey
1¼ cups sugar
1 teaspoon vanilla extract
2 tablespoons butter
3 cups whole pecans or walnuts

sweet pastry
Sweet pastry shell (see recipe on page 110)

PREPARATION
1. Pour the heavy cream into a small saucepan and warm over low heat.

2. In a large saucepan on low heat, add the water, honey, sugar, and vanilla. Stir until the sugar has dissolved, then increase the heat to medium high. Boil the sugar syrup until it has a deep amber hue (about 5 minutes).

3. Add the butter to the mixture and stir; it will bubble.

4. Add the warm cream slowly in a steady stream and stir. Continue to boil, stirring frequently (about 5 minutes). When the mixture looks like liquid caramel, remove it from the heat. Coat the nuts in the caramel mixture and set aside for 10 minutes to cool.

5. Preheat oven to 375°F.

6. Pour the caramel mixture into the sweet pastry shell.

7. Bake in oven for 20 minutes, until caramel bubbles and the crust is golden.

8. Remove from oven and cool on rack. Cool in pan for at least an hour before serving.

9. Remove from tart pan and serve.

Naturally Sweetened Ricotta
serves 6

This smooth and creamy dessert is delicious plain or garnished with fruit or caramelized chestnuts.

INGREDIENTS
 2 cups ricotta (see recipe on page 121)
 ½ cup heavy cream
 ⅓ cup honey or maple syrup (add more for desired sweetness)
 1 teaspoon vanilla extract
 1 cup marinated fresh berries, caramelized chestnuts, or roasted pears or apples

PREPARATION
 1. In a food processor, blend the ricotta, 1/4 cup of heavy cream, honey, and vanilla extract until smooth. If you desire a thinner, smoother consistency then slowly add more cream. Cover and place in the refrigerator for at least 1 hour.

 2. Garnish with marinated fresh berries, caramelized chestnuts, or roasted pears (see page 118).

Marinated Summer Berries
2 cups

INGREDIENTS
 2 cups of berries (blueberries, cherries, raspberries, strawberries, or mixed berries), cleaned
 ¼ cup Amaretto or Grand Marnier liqueur (optional)
 1 tablespoon sugar
 ½ lemon, juiced

PREPARATION
 1. Toss fruit, liqueur, sugar, and lemon juice in large bowl to combine. Cover and refrigerate for at least 1 hour.

Caramelized Chestnuts
1 cup

INGREDIENTS
 1 pound chestnuts (fresh or frozen), cooked and peeled
 3 tablespoon butter
 ½ teaspoon vanilla
 3 tablespoon honey or maple syrup

PREPARATION
 1. If using fresh chestnuts, preheat oven to 400°F. Score chestnuts with an X (on the bottom) and roast on a sheet pan until tender, approximately 20-25 minutes. Peel when cool.

 2. In a large ovenproof skillet over medium heat, melt the butter, then add vanilla and sweetener. Add the chestnuts and sauté for 10 minutes, turning frequently to coat with sauce. Transfer pan to oven and roast for 15 minutes, until browned.

 3. Serve warm with vanilla ice cream or naturally sweetened ricotta.

ᴗ References ᴗ

This section includes additional resources for a deeper understanding of the impact of your food choices. Please visit our website at michigansguidetolocalcooking.com for more detailed local references.

LOCATE LOCAL FOODS

Eat Well
eatwellguide.com

Eat Wild
eatwild.com

Farm Locator
rodaleinstitute.org/farm_locator

Food Routes
foodroutes.org

Local Harvest
localharvest.com

Locavores
locavores.com

Michigan MarketMaker
mimarketmaker.msu.edu

Michigan Farm Marketing and Agri-tourism Association
michiganfarmfun.com

Michigan Organic Food and Farming Alliance (MOFFA)
moffa.org

Michigan Farmer's Market Association (MIFMA)
farmersmarkets.msu.edu

National Cooperative Grocers Association
ncga.coop

Pick Your Own
pickyourown.org

The Sustainable Table
sustainabletable.org

CONSUMER ADVOCACY

American Farmland Trust
farmland.org

Environmental Working Group
ewg.org

People for the Ethical Treatment of Animals
peta.org

LOCAL FIRST ORGANIZATIONS

Buy Local Kalamazoo
buylocalkalamazoo.org

Capitol Area Local First
capitalarealocalfirst.com

Jackson Buy Local First
jxnlocalfirst.com

Local First
LocalFirst.com

Taste the Local Difference
LocalDifference.org

Think Local First
thinklocalfirst.net

Western Michigan FRESH
nacredata.info/wmi

FOOD CERTIFICATION

American Grassfed Association
americangrassfed.org

Animal Welfare Approved
animalwelfareapproved.org

Fair-trade Certified
transfairusa.org

Fair-trade Labelling Organizations International
fairtrade.net

Humane Farm Animal Care
certifiedhumane.org

TransFair USA
transfairusa.org

FOOD SECURITY/POLICY

Center for Economic Security
center4economicsecurity.org

Center for Food Safety
truefoodnow.org

Community Food Security Coalition
foodsecurity.org

The Food Trust
thefoodtrust.org

Food & Water Watch
foodandwaterwatch.org

Institute for Agriculture and Trade Policy
iatp.org

International Food Policy Research Institute
ifpri.org

Pesticide Action Network North America
panna.org

Seafood Choices Alliance
seafoodchoices.com

Seafood Watch
mbayaq.org/cr/seafoodwatch.asp

GOVERNMENT AGENCIES

U.S. Environmental Protection Agency
epa.gov

Food and Agriculture Organization of the United Nations
fao.org

U.S. Department of Agriculture (USDA)
usda.gov

USDA Farmer's Markets
ams.usda.gov/AMSv1.0

U.S. Food and Drug Administration
fda.gov

USDA National Agricultural Library
nal.usda.gov

USDA National Organic Program
ams.usda.gov/AMSv1.0/NOP

USDA Nutrition Assistance Programs
fns.usda.gov/fns

SUSTAINABLE FARMING

American Community Garden Association
communitygarden.org

Biodynamic Farming
biodynamics.com

The Ecological Farming Association
eco-farm.org

International Society of Organic Agricultural Research
www.isofar.org

McGill University Ecological Agriculture Projects and Organic library
eap.mcgill.ca

National Gardening Association
garden.org

National Sustainable Agriculture Coalition
sustainableagriculture.net

The National Sustainable Agriculture Information Service
attra.org

National Family Farm Coalition
nffc.net

The Organic Consumers Association
organicconsumers.org

Organic Farming Research Foundation
ofrf.org

The Research Institute of Organic Agriculture
fibl.org/english/index.php

The Sustainable Agriculture Research and Education
sare.org

The Alliance for Better Food and Farming
sustainweb.org

University of California, Davis Sustainable Agriculture Research and Food Education
sarep.ucdavis.edu

University of Wales Agroecology and Organic Farming Research
irs.aber.ac.uk

Washington State University Center for Sustaining Agriculture and Natural Resources
csanr.wsu.edu

OTHER ORGANIZATIONS

American Society for Nutrition
nutrition.org

EcoTrust
ecotrust.org

The Ethicurean
ethicurean.com

Food First
foodfirst.org

Food, Quality & Health
organicfqhresearch.org

The Food Project
thefoodproject.org

National Farm to School Network
farmtoschool.org

Sea Grant Michigan
miseagrant.umich.edu

Slow Food USA
slowfoodusa.org

Tufts University Friedman School of Nutrition Science and Policy
nutrition.tufts.edu

Whole Health MD.com
wholehealthmd.com

Worldwatch Institute
worldwatch.org

BOOKS

Animal, Vegetable, Miracle: A Year of Food Life. Kingsolver, Barbara, with Steven L. Hopp and Camille Kingsolver. (2007). New York: Harper Collins.

The Busy Person's Guide to Preserving Food: Easy Step-by-Step Instructions for Freezing, Drying and Canning. Chadwick, Janet. (1995). Massachusetts: Storey Publishing.

Coming Home to Eat: The Pleasures and Politics of Local Foods. Nabhan, Gary Paul. (2002). New York: W. W. Norton and Co.

Eat Where You Live. Bendrick, Lou. (2008). Seattle: Skipstone Books.

Food Politics: How the Food Industry Influences Nutrition and Health. Nestle, Marion. (2002). California: University of California Press.

Omnivore's Dilemma: A Natural History of Four Meals. Pollan, Michael. (2006). *The* New York: Penguin Press.

One Man, One Woman and A Raucous Year of Eating Locally. Smith. Alisa, and J. B. MacKinnon. (2007). New York: Harmony Books.

Slow Food Nation: Why Our Food Should Be Good, Clean, and Fair, Petrini, Carlo. (2007). New York: Rizzoli.

Slow Food Revolution: A New Culture for Eating and Living, Petrini, Carlo. (2006). New York: Rizzoli.

FILMS/DOCUMENTARIES

End of the Line: Directed by Rupert Murray (2009).

Fast Food Nation: Directed by Richard Linklater, written by Eric Schlosser (2006).

Fresh: Directed by Ana Sophia Jonas (2009).

The Garden, Directed by Scott Hamiltion Kennedy (2009).

Food Fight, Directed by Chris Taylor (2008).

Food Inc.: Directed by Robert Kenner (2009).

The Future of Food: Directed by Deborah Koons Garcia (2004).

King Corn: Directed by Aaron Woolf, Written by Ian Cheney and Curtis Ellis (2007).

To Market to Market to Buy a Fat Pig: Cast Rick Sebak (2007).

The Meaning of Food: (PBS 3 part series) Directed by Maria Gargiulo, Vivian Kleiman, Karin Williams (2004).

No impact Man: Laura Gabbert, Justin Schein (2009).

Our Daily Bread: Directed by Nikolaus Geyrhalter (2005).

The Real Dirt on Farmer John: Directed by Taggart Siegel (2005).

Tapped, Directed by Stephanie Soechtig, Jason Lindsey (2009).

What's On Your Plate?, Directed by Catherine Gund (2009).

What's Organic About Organic? Directed by Shelly Rogers (2011).

Index

Notes

Susan's lifelong affair with food began at the budding age of two while digging, planting and harvesting in the family vegetable garden. A few years later, she became a self-proclaimed sous chef, assisting her grandmother and her paisanos in the kitchen making pizzas at Clemente's Bar and Restaurant in Lincoln Park. Her Italian grandmother often prepared homemade, traditional Roman dishes from scratch using fresh, local foods. From a young age, Susan frequented farmers markets with her father, and the family would create fresh meals – her father prepared the meats and her mother prepared the veggies. She was always surrounded by good food. This is her foundation for the love of fresh local foods, and the philosophy that enjoying food and healthy eating are one in the same. "Let your food be your medicine and let your medicine be your food." - Hippocrates

Susan developed her passion further by attending both culinary and pastry schools, learning from internationally renowned master chef instructors. She attended the culinary program at Grand Rapids Community College, Grand Rapids, Michigan, and The French Pastry School (L'Art de la Pâtisserie), Chicago, Illinois. Susan most recently attended Kookoolan Farms cheese-making program in Oregon. All of her training prepared her to create her own recipes, as well as prepare and style food for final presentation.

Susan's professional background includes art direction, marketing, photography and writing for a variety of industries. She recently earned a Master of Professional Communication degree from Westminster College in Salt Lake City, Utah. She also earned a Bachelor of Fine Arts degree from The School of the Art Institute of Chicago with an emphasis on photography and design.

Susan is a member of The Farmers Market Coalition, The Michigan Farmers Market Association, Portland Culinary Alliance and Slow Food.

Susan's recent pastimes include visiting farms and farmers, exploring markets, savoring local beers and wines, and learning about and consuming as much fresh local food as possible.

To find out more about the project please visit the supplemental website at www.michigansguidetolocalcooking.com.

orange whisk
books